THE
47 RONIN
STORY

THE
47 RONIN
STORY

John Allyn

TUTTLE PUBLISHING
Tokyo • Rutland, Vermont • Singapore

First published in 2006 by Tuttle Publishing, an imprint of Periplus
Editions (HK) Ltd., with editorial offices at 364 Innovation Drive, North
Clarendon, Vermont 05759.

Library of Congress Catalog Card Number: 70-121274

ISBN-13: 978-0-8048-3827-6
ISBN-10: 0-8048-3827-5
ISBN: 4-8053-0871-0 (for sale in Japan only)

Distributed by:

North America
Tuttle Publishing
364 Innovation Drive
North Clarendon, VT 05759-9436
Tel: (802) 773-8930; Fax: (802) 773-6993
Email: info@tuttlepublishing.com
Website: www.tuttlepublishing.com

Japan
Tuttle Publishing
Yaekari Building, 3rd Floor
5-4-12 Ōsaki, Shinagawa-ku, Tokyo
Japan 141-0032
Tel: (03) 5437-0171; Fax: (03) 5437-0755
Email: tuttle-sales@gol.com

Asia Pacific
Berkeley Books Pte. Ltd.
130 Joo Seng Road #06-01/03
Singapore 368357
Tel: (65) 6280-1330; Fax: (65) 6280-6290
Email: inquiries@periplus.com.sg
Website: www.periplus.com

10 09 08 07 06   5 4 3 2 1

Printed in the United States of America

Contents

Among flowers, the cherry blossom;
among men, the samurai.

— Japanese proverb

Preface

JAPAN WAS A COUNTRY IN TURMOIL at the beginning of the 18th century. It was a time of pageantry and corruption in the Shogun's court in Edo (now Tokyo) and of riotous gaiety in the pleasure quarters of ancient Kyoto, shuttered away from the world of social restraint. The arts flourished; the popular theater was born. Because the merchant class was rising in power it was also the beginning of the end of privilege for the professional warriors, or samurai, who felt their loss keenly, especially since they held the business of money-making in contempt.

In the midst of such bewildering change, eruptions of violence were not unknown. They came most often in the form of rice riots by the farmers who were taxed beyond endurance by the Shogun, the military ruler of all Japan. That they did not occur more often among the samurai was a tribute to the thoroughness of their training and their remarkable self-discipline.

But even a samurai could be pushed too far. Especially a rash young lord forced into contact with the effete and degenerate ways of the court.

It happened in 1701 in Edo. In a moment of anger and frustration, Lord Asano of Ako lashed out at a corrupt court official and set in motion a chain of events that terminated in one of the bloodiest vendettas in Japan's feudal history. These events shocked the country and brought the Shogun himself to a legal and moral impasse. When it was all over, Japan had a new set of heroes—the forty-seven ronin, or ex-samurai, of Ako.

The historical facts of their deed are plain; the details are hazy. Celebrated in song, story, drama, and motion pictures, many widely differing versions have been produced.

This novel is intended to give an account in English of what might have happened in those colorful days when Japan was secluded from the rest of the world and the old traditions still governed the lives of men.

— John Allyn

Chapter One

MARCH 13, 1701.

The sun completed its route over the Pacific and began to set, the waters reddening around the islands of Japan. To the southwest, on a path near the Inland Sea, a tall man on an unkempt stallion shielded his eyes from the glare as he rode tight-lipped through the pines.

His name was Oishi; he was the chief retainer of the Asano clan, the rulers of this hilly domain. He was returning to the castle at Ako after an all-day horseback tour of the castle town with his master's little daughter, who rode beside him on a pony with a tangled mane.

They made a strange pair. Oishi was a handsome man in his early forties with a high-domed forehead, a square jaw, and an air of quiet authority. His topknot, pleated *hakama* skirt, and two swords identified him as a samurai, a member of the warrior class. The child was petite and vivacious, bright as a butterfly in kimono and obi. Yet, in spite of their differences, each was comfortable in the other's presence. The girl was freed from the strict discipline her parents imposed on her; Oishi was freer with a child, especially someone else's, to relax his official manner and even joke a little.

At the moment, as their shabby horses jogged homeward, there was less conversation between them than usual. Oishi was appalled at what he had seen in the town, and the little girl respected his silence.

All his life Oishi had heard the Buddhist edicts against violence and cruelty, but in practice they had always been tempered with common sense. Sometimes one had to kill to defend oneself against an enemy, or, in the case of animals, to get food. Personally, he had always deplored the cruelty in tournaments where dogs were brought down by spears or arrows and he had no objection to such sport being abolished. But the Shogun's new Life Preservation Laws went much too far. Animals were now apparently more privileged than humans and this topsy-turvy manner of thinking had brought the whole country to the brink of economic chaos.

In the town Oishi had seen once thriving farmers begging for jobs because they were not allowed to fight back against the pests that destroyed their crops. Foxes, badgers, birds, and insects ran rampant in the fields while those who had planted the seed stood by helplessly.

Oishi knew that poultry was secretly being sold in the back rooms of some otherwise respectable shops, but on the whole violations of the law were few. Not only was the administrative machinery of the Shogun's government extremely effective in catching lawbreakers, but the penalty for injuring any living thing was severe. For taking the life of an animal, the punishment was the execution of the "criminal" himself.

There were others who were as badly off as the farmers. The occupations of hunter, trapper, and tanner had become obsolete and these men, too, were crowding the towns, seeking some way to support their families. To their consternation, they found that jobs were scarce and food prices high, boosted out of reach of the common people by the scant supply of farm products. The only commodity seemingly available at a low price was a young girl to sleep with, due to the growing number of farmers' daughters who had been sold into the brothels to tide their families over the bad times.

As always, Oishi had skirted the so-called pleasure quarters when touring the town with Lord Asano's daughter, but now the houses of prostitution were increasing so fast that they spread right out onto the main road and were impossible to avoid. Shocking was the word for it, and he was certainly going to bring it to his master's attention when he returned.

As yet his own class had not felt the economic pinch—the samurai were paid out of funds that came from selling the rice grown on their lords' fiefs at the going high prices—but their lives had been affected by the Shogun's edict in other ways.

There was no more archery practice or competition, because they could not pluck goosefeathers for their arrows. There was no more falconry because all the birds had been set at liberty and even the Shogun's Master of Hawks had been discharged. Horsemanship was becoming a lost art because the horses' hooves could not be pared or their manes clipped under penalty of banishment. But worst of all, in Oishi's mind, was the general laxity of morals that was spreading from the Shogun's capital down into the provinces.

As the son of a samurai, Oishi had spent his childhood in the study of Confucian ethics as part of the necessary training of a soldier who must learn loyalty as well as fierceness on the field of battle. Because of this, he was shocked at reports that the dancing and play-acting that overran Shogun Tsunayoshi's capital at Edo (Tokyo) was beginning to have a softening effect on the samurai quartered there. He had even heard rumors that samurai had been seen in the Kabuki theaters of Kyoto, the city of pleasure as well as of temples, but these he found hard to believe.

Such things had been going on for some time, but Oishi had not been aware of just how bad things had gotten in town until today. He began to compose in his mind the report he would make to Lord Asano, and as he thought of her father he turned toward the little girl riding beside him. She smiled at him but then her expression became more serious. She, too, had noticed a change in the countryside.

"Uncle," she asked him, "why are all the farms so messy looking? They're none of them kept up well at all. Don't you think you ought to report the farmers to my father for not properly doing their jobs?"

Oishi laughed heartily and she was reassured before he spoke that things were not as bad as they seemed. "Let's not blame the farmers until we know their side of it, too, shall we?"

"But what excuse could they have for neglecting their fields so?"

"It's not because they want to neglect them, little daughter. It's the animals they're forbidden to kill by the Life Preservation Laws that are ruining the land."

"But why are we forbidden to kill the animals—especially those that annoy us so?"

"Because the Shogun has said it is wrong to take the life of an animal and because we are loyal to our master, your father, and would not think of bringing shame on him by disobeying the orders of *his* lord, the Shogun."

"But why did he make this hard law in the first place?"

Oishi sighed. As much as the law hurt, he could understand Tsunayoshi's reasons for promulgating it.

"Because more than anything else in the world he wants a child. A sweet, pretty child like you. He lost one you know—a little boy four years old who died. And his priest has told him that in order to have another, he must atone for some sin committed in a previous life—one in which he most likely wantonly destroyed some living thing. You've seen that we don't use dogs in our tournaments any more—that's because our Shogun was born in the Year of the Dog and to kill a dog is now punishable by death."

"Even if one should attack you?"

Oishi mused for a moment. "In that case it might be all right—but it would be a good idea to have witnesses that the dog took the first bite."

He smiled at her and the little girl smiled back, but she was not sure whether he was joking or not. She decided she would ask her father about it when he got home from Edo.

With a shout she kicked her little feet into her horse's flanks and lurched into a gallop. "I'll race you home," she cried, already ten lengths ahead, her long hair flying.

Oishi gave the fierce cry of the attacking warrior and galloped after her. He maintained the distance between them, and together they moved over the winding road and up the final hill. At the top they came in sight of the castle, far below in the middle of a large plain, strategically located so that invaders could not approach unseen. It was always a spectacular sight with its high stone walls and white tile-topped towers, but on this occasion neither of them paused to appreciate the view.

The sinking sun was throwing long clutching shadows behind them as they raced down the hill toward the gate. It crossed Oishi's mind that when the same sun rose again in the morning it would be the beginning of Lord Asano's last day in Edo. He hoped all was going well at the ceremonies in the Shogun's capital where the etiquette was so unfamiliar and demanding. Lord Asano was not noted for his patience and the less he had to participate, the better. Anyway, he would soon know the whole story. As the little girl entered the gate, well ahead of him as always, and he followed to receive the salutes of the sentries, the thought came again: tomorrow would be the last day.

Chapter Two

DAWN BROKE COLDLY OVER EDO, the capital city of old Japan. It was to be a bleak, sunless day. The chill wind that rolled down from the high snow-covered mountains rattled the rain doors of the farmhouses on the outskirts, then lifted a billow of dust along the post road from the southwest as it entered the city.

On its way it picked up the stench of human excreta from the rice fields, the incenselike odor of smoke from the charcoal fires in the kitchens of early-rising housewives, and finally the saltiness of the briny sea off the flat waters of Edo Bay.

At ground level the wind lost its force in the narrow alleyways that twisted through the maze of flimsy wooden structures that were both homes and places of business to nearly seven hundred thousand merchants and artisans. Above the tile-topped roofs it continued gustily on toward the higher ground in the center of the city, dipped to cross a rock-lined moat, and became random among the watchtowers and palaces of Edo Castle where the Shogun Tsunayoshi, the supreme ruler of the land, held his court.

As it moved pungently, invisibly along, the wind also acquired a sound. Sweeping through a graveyard and the public execution grounds, it startled a mongrel cur and set him howling, which in turn set off others around him until in no time the air was filled with the dismal wailing of a thousand stray dogs. The sound swelled and became more menacing as it forced its way into the hovels of beggars and the mansions of the nobility, to enter the sleeping ears of poor and rich alike....

Lord Asano, Daimyo of the Province of Ako, still boyishly good-looking at thirty-five, was riding with his chief retainer Oishi through a misty landscape, running down a deadly wild boar that was menacing the farmers. As they moved into the ever thickening fog, an eerie hum began to throb in Lord Asano's ears and his horse reacted nervously. Behind him, Oishi pulled up to a prudent halt, but Lord Asano impatiently spurred his own mount forward and disappeared from sight.

"My Lord Asano!" Oishi called in sudden anxiety. "Come back, come back!"

But Lord Asano's stubborn pride would not let him turn back and he pressed on through the dense vacuum of the fog until the unearthly sound became a screech and then a deafening howl. He felt a stab of terror as he was sucked into the sound and lost all sense of direction. In the dazzling white of the fog he was sightless and felt himself lose his balance and start to fall. The howling grew louder and he knew he must fight for his life to escape the demons that were waiting to devour him. He cried out for help and in that instant he woke in his villa near the Shogun's castle to hear the howling of the dogs of Edo fading away on the wind that had brought it.

"Husband!" his wife cried out as she raised herself to watch him struggling to draw his sword from the scabbard beside him. "What's the matter?"

Fully awake now, he shook his head and threw down the sword. "The dogs," he muttered. "The damned dogs."

"Go back to sleep," she said, as a soothing smile came over her pretty round face. "You should be used to them by now."

"I'll never get used to them, or to anything else about this miserable place."

"Only one more day," she reminded him. "Then we'll go home to Ako and our daughter."

"One more day," he repeated in a tone that was both forlorn and hopeful. "One more rotten day."

He tried to go back to sleep but his heart was still pounding from his nightmare and his eyes would not close. He watched restlessly as the light of dawn slipped through the window shutters and crept across the *tatami* mats to his bed on the floor. Lord Asano sighed and rolled out of the heavy quilts to stand shivering for a moment in his underclothes, then put on a padded robe to slide open the paper-paneled door and step into the cold corridor beyond.

He walked with long steps over the slick wood, darkly polished by the passage of countless stockinged feet. At one side the corridor was lined by pillars of fragrant cedar separated by painted *shoji* panels; on the other side rain doors sheltered it from the garden outside, and Lord Asano shivered as they rattled in the wind and he imagined he heard again the dogs of his dreams.

He opened the sliding door to the kitchen and stepped in. It was a large room, floored with rough boards, with a clay-lined central fireplace sunk in the floor. Here, two topknotted samurai from his retinue sat warming themselves, and as he approached and muttered a greeting they scrambled to their knees and bowed low.

Kataoka, the younger of the two, wiry, with a face like a playful monkey, started to exchange a pleasantry with his master, but changed his mind when he saw his face. Lord Asano was tense by nature, but this morning he appeared more so than usual and Kataoka knew when to keep quiet. The other man, a fierce-looking warrior in his fifties named Hara, was sleepy eyed and not so perceptive; he merely followed Kataoka's lead in sinking back into a cross-legged position by the fire as their master sat down.

"You needn't have gotten up so early," Lord Asano told Hara. "Kataoka is the only escort I'll need today, and all he can do is stand outside and look up at the castle towers and dream of home."

Hara grunted and his glittering eyes showed briefly, then his sleepy lids drooped again and he lifted his rice bowl close to his face to eat. Kataoka bobbed his head and grinned his monkey smile of pleasure at the honor of being his lord's sole companion on such an auspicious occasion, then coughed as the smoke from the fire blew into his face. Lord Asano reached for the teapot hanging over the fire, but the smoke stung his eyes and he cursed as he flung the kettle back onto its hook.

"Mimura!" he called, and a sudden shuffling in the pantry told him that Mimura had heard.

The servant, a tall, awkward young fellow, entered in great haste and bowed low to his master. As he raised his eyes he saw that the smoke was going everywhere except out the opening in the roof made for it, and he quickly reached into the pit to pull out the green sticks that were causing the trouble.

"Who put those in there?" said Lord Asano sharply. "You know better than that, Mimura. Can't you help get this miserable day off to a better start?"

Mimura apologized in a profusion of polite phrases and muttered under his breath about the stupidity of the new fire boy. Then he crossed to the pantry door and called out.

There was an unexplained delay and he called again. This time he was answered by the appearance of the fire boy's head in the doorway, a great shock of black unruly hair over an impudent face. Mimura bawled him out for his carelessness, but if he expected an apology he was disappointed. The boy, in a loud raucous voice, told Mimura that if he was so particular he could make the fire himself and abruptly withdrew, slamming the door shut behind him.

The men at the fire were shocked at this display and Hara was so incensed he leaped to his feet and pulled his long sword.

"What does he mean by talking to one of our servants like that?" he exclaimed as he started for the pantry door.

"No, wait," said Lord Asano in a weary voice of authority. "He's only a boy. Besides, you'll get yourself in trouble if you harm him. The laws are different here; we can't behave as we would at home."

"But to insult your servant is to insult you, too," Hara insisted. "I should at least slit his tongue for him if you won't let me take off his head."

"Sit down—sit down and drink your tea. You've got to get used to the ways of Edo. Here the comings and goings of daimyo from the provinces are so commonplace that they hold no terror for even a lowly fire boy."

Hara, still muttering, put away his sword and sat down. He watched carefully as Mimura opened the pantry door and stepped through. In a moment there came the sounds of a slap and a yelp of pain, and Hara smiled as Kataoka laughed out loud.

"That'll take care of the young monkey," he shouted and made the most monkeylike grin at his command. The others smiled and Kataoka was pleased that he had helped his master forget his troubles, if only temporarily.

"I wish all the Edoites were so easily handled," said Lord Asano as he sighed and helped himself to some rice. "But I'm afraid that's not the case. Especially with those who have a little authority."

The two samurai exchanged glances. They knew what their master meant.

"These court dandies all ought to have their heads removed," growled Hara, and Kataoka nodded in agreement. "They talk and dress like women and are just as troublesome."

"Anyway, it'll all be over after today," Lord Asano said. "Then we can go home to Ako and forget this place. Think what it must have been like in the old days when daimyo like my father had to stay here half of every year."

The others agreed that the present arrangement was better than that, and finished eating their rice. Hara looked sorrowfully into the bottom of his bowl and Lord Asano knew what he was thinking.

"At least in the old days we had a little meat and fish to go with our rice, eh, Hara? Well, maybe we will again some day if the Shogun's Life Preservation Laws are ever rescinded. They may benefit the animals, but they don't do us humans much good." He put his bowl down and sighed again. "Most of the laws around here seem only meant to torment us. And the court's rules of etiquette are completely beyond me. If only I didn't have to depend for instructions on someone like Kira!"

He spat out the name like a curse and again Hara and Kataoka exchanged worried looks. They knew he would not elaborate on this subject—it would be beneath him to discuss his personal grievances with them—but from what they had heard they knew that Kira, the court Master of Ceremonies, was making his life miserable. And they also knew there was nothing they could do about it.

Kira's name stuck in Lord Asano's mind like a bone in his throat. He had never known such a miserable time in the capital before, and it was a place he had never enjoyed visiting. This time, however, he was an unwilling participant in the official proceedings instead of a mere spectator and was thrown into much closer contact with the Shogun's underlings. Kira was not even of daimyo rank, having no fief of his own and being ruler of nothing. But the fact that he had been sent to Kyoto some years before to study ceremonial procedure at the court of the Emperor gave him prestige and power that he had since used to good advantage in exacting bribes from those who had to depend on his tutelage.

Lord Asano had written about Kira only the night before in a letter to his chief retainer Oishi. Although Oishi was slightly older, he was less experienced in the ways of the court at Edo than his master, and Lord Asano was able to express his feelings about Kira in the guise of offering advice on how to behave in the capital.

"Kira is the man to watch out for," he had written. "He enjoys the confidence of the Shogun and appears to be a faithful servant, but in truth he is an unscrupulous bribetaker and uses his office solely for his own ends. There is seemingly no way of dealing with such men except to play their game, but this I refuse to do. Consequently, Kira is giving me a rough time of it, even with only one day to go. Regardless of what happens, however, I will not pay Kira for his services, which are supposed to be supplied by the court. This may be a stubborn attitude, but as far as I am concerned it is the only honorable one for a samurai to take. I do not expect that I alone can turn back the wave of decadence that seems to have engulfed the court, but I can try to hold my head above the dirty water as long as there is a breath left in me."

He wondered if Oishi would understand. In Ako there was nothing to compare with the Shogun's court and he himself would not have believed such corruption existed if he had not seen it with his own eyes. Still, Oishi thought like a true samurai and could appreciate his feelings. He doubted that his words would ever be taken as practical advice, but at least it was good to get the matter off his chest.

He finished eating and rose with a sigh.

"Time to put on my 'clown suit,'" he told Kataoka, and together they moved out of the room as Hara sat scowling at the forces that were troubling his master.

At the castle Kira was up early, too. As Master of Ceremonies for all court functions he was obliged to be impeccable in dress as well as in manner and he took pains to maintain high standards. The robes laid out for him were similar in style to those the visiting daimyo and officials of the court would be wearing, but the color scheme he had chosen of dead black with a huge white crest on each oversized sleeve guaranteed him a more striking appearance than any of them.

Although scarcely middle aged, Kira affected to be older because he thought it added to his dignity. Except for two deep frown lines creased into his brow, however, his face was free of wrinkles and his heavy-set body was hard and agile. His teeth, in accord with the latest fashion, were blackened so that when he opened his mouth to speak, his listeners saw only a dark, toothless hole.

Strangely enough, for one in such exalted if temporary power over the daimyo of the land, Kira was worried about the behavior of one of them. Lord Asano was of the old school of samurai and did not seem to realize that in this modern age bribes in the right pockets would do him more good than meaningless affirmations of loyalty to the Shogun. And for this reason he constituted a threat to Kira's way of life.

For three days now Kira had tried by flattery, by hints, and finally by insults to convey the idea to Lord Asano that it was customary to bestow gifts of money on the court Master of Ceremonies for his services. But Lord Asano had continued to ignore him, and Kira's fear was that if he got away with this act of ingratitude it could set a bad precedent. Kira's stipend as a court officer was not large and he had no desire to lose any extra benefits because of Lord Asano's stubbornness. Somehow, there must be a way to get to his man. He had never failed in the past to get what he wanted from these noble young fools and he was determined that this time would be no exception.

His thoughts were interrupted by the arrival of a breathless servant with the announcement that the Shogun Tsunayoshi wanted to see him immediately. He hurried to put on his robes, cursing because he could not finish dressing in the leisurely way he had planned. Then he hastened out the door and across the palace grounds to the inner palace, wondering all the while what could be troubling the Shogun this early in the morning.

In the twenty-first year of his reign, Tsunayoshi had every reason to be contented. There had been no uprisings against his office for several decades, mainly because his ancestors had been so thorough in uniting the country, first by conquest and then by assigning fiefs in strategic locations to blood relatives. His predecessors had also done him a favor by expelling all foreigners, except for one small group of Dutch traders on an island at the extreme southern tip of the country. The Christian influence had lingered for some time, even after the expulsion, but sixty years before, at Shimabara, the last large-scale massacre of such deviants had left the country free of even this minor annoyance.

Now, after years of peace, the towns were growing, the merchants were prospering, and the arts were flourishing. It was true that the price of rice was going up, due to short supplies from the farmers who seemed strangely unable to get the most from their land, but on the whole Tsunayoshi was free from any pressing problems of state. But that is not to say that he had no problems at all.

As Kira entered, puffing more heavily than was really necessary, he could see that Tsunayoshi was indeed in an anxious state. Kira bowed as low as his robes would permit and then raised his eyes to the tall, thin man in his fifties, who was pacing mincingly up and down the ornate reception room.

Tsunayoshi's concern, it turned out, was not with any pressing matters of state, but rather with how the performance of his dancing group would be received at the ceremonies. He had selected and coached the boys himself and was concerned that they give a good account of themselves. So much so that he had decided another rehearsal was in order and this was why he had summoned Kira. He wanted the boys assembled in the Hall of the Thousand Mats as quickly as possible so they could run through their dance once more before the distinguished guests arrived.

"You don't know how much this means to me," he told Kira, with a womanish wave of his kimono sleeve. "I've worked *so* hard to make this performance a success—it's just *got* to come off perfectly!"

Kira bowed his head. "I sympathize with Your Excellency but I'm sure you have nothing to worry about. The ceremonies will be carried out smoothly as always."

"The ceremonies, yes—but the dance, that's what's important to me. This is something new for such an occasion and if it fails, I'll be laughed at by everyone."

"No one would think of doing such a thing," Kira reassured him.

"The experts will laugh behind my back even if they don't say anything," Tsunayoshi said knowingly. "But enough of that—everything else is all right, isn't it? No problems at your end, I hope?"

"There are always problems, Your Excellency, but nothing I can't handle myself."

"Good," smiled the Shogun. "That's what I like to hear from my courtiers. I wish they were all as efficient as you."

Kira smiled back at him, revealing his blackened teeth. "All I know was learned from your example."

He bowed and started to leave, then hesitated and turned back in feigned reluctance. "There is one rather troublesome young daimyo, but I hope I will be able to correct his awkwardness before it embarrasses us."

"You mean Asano, don't you? I've noticed that he doesn't seem as much at ease as the others. Do you want me to speak to him?"

"No—I don't think that will be necessary. He'll be all right once I get him to understand his proper place."

"Yes—well, I leave that to you. But get those young boys over here in a hurry, will you?"

"I will obey," Kira answered formally with a bow, and hurried away as fast as his elaborate robes would permit. He knew from experience that Tsunayoshi was not long on patience.

Dressed in his ceremonial robes, with every detail of his costume checked and double-checked against the rules of dress for the court, Lord Asano was carried to the palanquin that was to take him to the Shogun's castle. Kataoka, also more splendidly dressed than usual, was about to give the order for the eight burly bearers to pick up their poles when Lord Asano's wife appeared in the doorway of the mansion and called out. Kataoka called to the bearers to wait, then stepped aside so his master could converse with his wife in privacy.

"Please," she said as she leaned in the window to him, "please promise me you'll keep your temper. Show the court of Edo that we from the country also know our place in society. Perhaps—perhaps it's not too late even now to put a few coins in the right palms..."

Lord Asano made a gesture of impatience, but his expression softened as he saw her concern. His words were reproving, but his manner was gentle.

"In solemn matters of this sort, giving more than a token gift to the court Master of Ceremonies would be a cheap and vulgar act and I refuse to stoop to such a level. My councilors agree..."

"Your councilors agree because you've already made up your own mind and they know it would be useless to oppose you. I can see that if you can't... At least promise me you'll take his instructions in good grace and not lose your temper, won't you?"

"I promise," he said, and satisfied that he meant it, she stepped back and forced a smile of farewell. Lord Asano now motioned to the waiting Kataoka and the bearers were given the signal to move out.

As they rounded the corner of the house Kataoka saw Hara watching them go and caught an unspoken warning in the big man's eyes: "Take good care of our master." Kataoka nodded as he passed and then Hara disappeared behind them.

They moved through a portion of the immense garden that surrounded the mansion and Lord Asano noticed that even though the trees were bare the grounds were still remarkably beautiful in the early morning light. There was no single distinguishing feature, only a total impression of natural serenity, meticulously planned by his grandfather at a time when there were still wars or threats of war and the daimyo were required to spend long periods in the capital. Now, of course, things were different. There had not been even a minor uprising for as long as Lord Asano could remember. It occurred to him, as it had many times before, that life must have been more exciting in grandfather's day when a sword was something to settle your differences with and not just a badge of rank.

The palanquin was carried briskly out the gate, Kataoka trotting alongside, but as they entered the din and crowds in the narrow alleys of the city the bearers were obliged to slow to a walking pace. Most of the tradesmen and shoppers gave way when they recognized the crested palanquin of a daimyo, but in the press of humanity not all noticed its presence, or pretended not to, and kept doggedly about their business until they were firmly pushed aside.

Lord Asano had never gotten used to this flocking together of the classes that one found in Edo. From the highest ranking nobles of the court to the lowest commoner, all gathered at this center of commerce to buy from the prospering merchants. There were other types present, too, including a few threadbare ronin, or masterless samurai. Farmers who could not make a go of it had come to the city to find work and there were plenty of these, proudly disdaining to ask for bread. At the opposite extreme were the professional beggars, calling loudly for alms in the cocky, Edo-like manner that recalled to Lord Asano the boy who had made such a mess of the fire that morning. He might be out of a job now but the chances were he was not worried. Anyone with his brass would require little apprenticeship to take to the streets to cry for handouts or to become a pseudoreligious mendicant and beg in the name of a nobler cause.

The din was overwhelming now, but over it there came another sound, a chant for the dead, and Kataoka directed the bearers to pull over to the side to let a funeral procession pass. Through the window of the palanquin Lord Asano could see that the funeral group consisted of only two men, both servants, and that the rough casket they carried slung from a pole between them was unusually small. Kataoka was standing perplexedly by the side of the palanquin when Lord Asano spoke and startled him.

"Not the best omen to begin the day with, eh, Kataoka?"

Kataoka turned to see that his master was not smiling and felt compelled to do something to alleviate his black mood. The servants with the casket had stopped their chanting now and as they came nearer one of them began to grumble about the load. In desperation, and also in annoyance at the man's bad manners, Kataoka called out to him.

"Ho! Your load is small enough. What are you complaining for? Can't you show more reverence for the dead?"

The servant laughed roughly at this and shouted to his companion. "The man wants to know why we don't show more reverence for our passenger. Shall I show him?"

"Sure," the other man responded. "Why not?"

By now they were abreast of the palanquin and they stopped to set the casket down in the middle of the alley. The servant who had spoken first came forward and smiled broadly at Kataoka, then winked and flipped open the lid of the box. In it lay the body of a small dog, cut almost in two in an accident. The servant winked at Kataoka again as the jostling crowd pressed close, all trying to see what was causing such interest.

"She was never treated so well in all her life," the servant yelled at Kataoka, who was momentarily at a loss for words.

"Where are you taking her?" he finally mumbled.

"To the burying grounds, of course. Where do you think? Don't you know the law says dogs have to be buried just like people? We're only carrying out the Shogun's orders."

He covered the box and moved back to the end of the pole.

"Well, the least you can do is carry them out without complaint," Kataoka told them both. "You don't seem to realize how lucky you are that our exalted Shogun was born under the sign of the dog." He paused for dramatic effect as they lifted the pole to their shoulders. "What do you think you'd be carrying if he'd been born under the sign of the horse?"

The two men laughed loudly, as did all those in the crowd who overheard, and Kataoka was pleased to see that even Lord Asano smiled. He chuckled at his own cleverness, then gave the bearers the order to move out and once again they were plunged into the tumultuous sea of humanity that flooded the street.

Inside the palanquin, Lord Asano was thinking about the dead dog. To him it was typical of the topsy-turvy world of

Edo that animals should be treated like humans. He knew he would never understand this place and wished again to be out of it. He sighed, then leaned forward to watch with more interest as the palanquin was carried out of the last alleyway and onto a broad street which paralleled the castle moat.

The waters of the moat were below street level at this point and barely visible. What was most apparent was the high wall of gigantic blocks of granite beyond the water, forming an insurmountable barrier around the unseen castle. Now the bearers turned and moved alongside the moat, jogging up a little hill toward an entrance gate which guarded a narrow high-flung bridge over the still waters below.

There were guards at the gate who came to attention as the palanquin approached. They were armed with lances and halberds which were held at the ready while Kataoka identified the party and stated the reasons for the visit. Then, waved on with a shout, they crossed the bridge into the grounds of the castle itself. On the right as they entered was a long wooden structure which quartered a full company of on-duty guards. The armed men outside it again challenged the palanquin and again Kataoka had to go through the formality of identification.

They proceeded at a measured walk, in accordance with security regulations, and next came to an outer castle where the nobles and their families lived, surrounded by the palaces and courts of lesser ranking officials in a square that constituted a small town in itself. There was little activity in the streets, however, as most of the nobles were inside preparing for the events of the day.

Past this, on higher ground, was the inner castle and official residence of the Shogun himself. It was surrounded by another moat and a thick wall of freestone like the granite one below. A drawbridge was positioned over the moat and Lord Asano's party moved even more slowly across it, their pace fixed by the court's immutable rules.

Inside the wall, wide ramparts of earth supported guard-houses several stories high at each corner of the enclosure. Above the castle itself a white tower rose aloft above all the other buildings, and at sight of this Lord Asano exchanged a quick understanding glance with Kataoka. It was this which reminded them both of home. It was a great square mass of stone and plaster with narrow white-barred windows and tiers of curving roofs zigzagging over one another to a high ridge on each end of which was a bronze fish with an uplift-ed tail. Although the castle in Ako was not this large or ornate, the tower design was similar and stirred both their memories.

At the entrance to the castle, the palanquin stopped and Lord Asano got out. He stepped directly onto a low wooden porch so there was no need for him to be lifted out by his bearers. His costume was brilliant green, and he made an expression of distaste as he looked down at himself. Outfits like this were one of his biggest problems in life at the capital. Besides a ridiculous hat that flopped over on one side and threatened to fall off if he inclined his head, he was strapped into a broad-shouldered *kamishimo* jacket that constricted his arm movements. But worst of all were the cumbersome trousers which Kataoka now hastened to adjust for Lord Asano's entrance into the castle.

The voluminous legs were overlong by several feet and were supposed to stretch out flatly behind the wearer for aes-thetic effect. This required great care in walking and Lord Asano, naturally impatient, felt hemmed in and vulnerable. He had a constant urge to kick holes in the legs and strut in his normal manner instead of mincing along like a woman in a tight kimono. Kataoka finished laying out the cloth so that his master was pointed in the right direction, then bowed deeply and withdrew. He would wait in the vicinity of the guard shack with the bearers until the ceremonies were over. He was not, of course, allowed to enter the castle under any circumstances. No one below the rank of daimyo was invited to the annual reception for the Emperor's envoys.

Lord Asano braced himself and started the walk to the door. Although it was only a short distance, it seemed to him interminable as he carefully lifted each foot, kicked it slightly forward, and took a step down onto the trouser legs themselves. There were only a couple of guards watching him at the moment, but Lord Asano walked as carefully for their benefit as he would have before the Shogun himself. He knew that Kira would goad him unmercifully if he made even one false step, and he was determined to show these Edoites that a samurai from the country could play their game.

As one of the guards held the door open, he entered the waiting room outside the enormous Hall of the Thousand Mats where the official ceremonies would be held. Inside he paused to let his eyes become accustomed to the dimmer light.

The waiting room was spacious and high ceilinged with gilded beams and carved pillars. As he stepped onto the gold-bordered mats, Lord Asano noticed that, even though he was early, there were several lords there ahead of him. All were dressed in court costume similar to his, differing in detail only to denote rank. One, in an outfit identical to his except that it was golden brown, looked pointedly at him and it was in this man's direction that he made his way.

Lord Daté of Yoshida, a trim athletic-looking fellow in his thirties, was Lord Asano's counterpart in rank and assignment. Both their names had been drawn by lot to be official representatives of the Shogun at this reception of the Emperor's envoys from Kyoto, an annual affair that represented one of the few contacts between the Emperor, who was ruler in name only, and the Shogun, whose recent ancestors had unified the country by military action and who was the actual head of the government.

Both Lord Asano and Lord Daté had tried to decline the honor on the grounds that they were unfamiliar with court etiquette, but neither had been successful. They had been put under Kira's wing to learn the protocol for the occasion and were completely dependent on him to coach them through their various functions. Daté had little trouble with Kira, however, while Lord Asano was constantly being ridiculed about his "country manners." Now, at the start of the final day, Lord Daté looked cool and complacent while his fellow participant was noticeably apprehensive.

"Good morning," Lord Asano said, with a perfunctory bow.

"Good morning, Lord Asano," smiled Daté. "You're early, aren't you?"

"So are you," retorted Lord Asano. "Maybe you're more nervous than you appear."

Daté laughed. "You're the nervous one. Anyone would think you were going into battle."

"I wish it were a battle," Lord Asano said testily. "I'm a country boy with no talent for getting along with these fancy-pants courtiers. Men like Kira," and he spoke the name distastefully, "are of lower rank than we, yet we are supposed to jump when they give the word." He shook his head. "I just don't seem to know my place here."

"I don't know why you should have so much trouble with Kira," said Daté with a sly smile. "He's treated me with respect, even though I'm as clumsy as you about the ceremonies."

Lord Asano looked at him warily. "Don't think I don't know your secret, Lord Daté. You knuckled under to his demands and have paid him off..."

"I did no such thing!" Daté interrupted angrily.

"Then your councilors did it for you and that doesn't reflect credit on you either—not to know what's going on in your own house!"

Daté's face reddened and he was about to respond in kind when the sliding doors to the hall within opened and Lord

Kira himself stepped ponderously out. He smiled conde-scendingly at the group in the waiting room, revealing his fashionably blackened teeth, and Lord Asano shuddered as he always did at such signs of decadence. The nuts chewed to achieve such an effect were expensive and he considered such practice the height of vulgarity, quite contrary to the tenets of frugality taught by Buddha and Confucius alike. In his view, Kira represented the epitome of all that was wrong with the court. He was corrupt, vain, and self-important—about as far from the traditional ideal of a samurai as it was possible to be.

Kira looked pointedly at Lord Asano after the customary bows of greeting had been exchanged, hoping for some sign of a change in attitude. Surely, he thought, there must be some way to get to this noble idiot. Perhaps stronger insults would be more effective with such a proud young man. At least it was worth one more try and there was no better time than the present. He knew he was safe; drawing a sword in the castle, no matter what the circumstances, was a capital offense.

As Kira started to move toward him, Lord Asano instinc-tively turned away in what could only be interpreted as a ges-ture of disdain. The black-clad Master of Ceremonies halted in surprise then angrily changed his course to approach Lord Daté instead. This rude act was the last straw and Kira, his blood rising, knew now that it was useless to go on trying to collect his bribe. He resolved that Lord Asano would pay for his incorruptibility—and his rudeness.

As Kira's instructions to Lord Daté went on, Lord Asano felt a tremendous depression settle over him. He knew that his own self-indulgence had once again cost him Kira's good will. If Kira neglected him now, he would be at a complete loss to know what to do during the ceremony. He felt a moment of panic as he anticipated the disgrace he would bring on his family name if he should commit some terrible breach of etiquette. After all, Kira was the recognized expert on such matters and the least he could do was be civil to the man, even if he despised him.

He was trying to compose some statement of apology when the outside door opened. His pulse quickened at the thought that it might be the Imperial envoys, but he breathed easier when he saw that it was only an attendant of the Shogun's mother who entered. He was a pop-eyed, plump little man named Kajikawa whom Lord Asano would ordinarily have ignored, but on this occasion he was astute enough not to reveal his true feelings. As Kajikawa looked timidly around the room, Lord Asano smiled encouragingly.

The smile worked and Kajikawa scurried over, sinking into an exaggerated bow of respect as he arrived. Then he lifted his head with a froggy smile...

"Lord Asano," he said in a lisping rush of words, "I have heard that there's been a change in the time schedule and I would like to know what it is so that I can tell our exalted Shogun's mother. If it wouldn't be too much trouble..." he finished on the correct note of uncertainty.

Lord Asano's eyes went involuntarily to Kira as the only one who could answer and was discomfited to find that Kira was smiling blackly back at him and had obviously heard the question.

"Don't bother to ask that dolt anything," Kira said loudly and in his grandest manner. "If it's a question about the ceremony, ask me or Lord Daté, or one of the servants—even they know more about what's going on than *Lord* Asano!"

Kajikawa's face turned red and his eyes popped wider than ever as he bowed uncertainly, then stood in indecision. Lord Asano had gone dead white and stood as stiffly as if he had been turned to stone. Kajikawa felt a sudden twinge of dread and moved away toward the sliding doors to the assembly hall. He did not want to humiliate Lord Asano any further by going to anyone else in the room, and decided to ask his question of one of the courtiers inside. He had started to open the door when he saw Lord Kira move majestically across the room to stop in front of Lord Asano and say something to him in low tones. He could not be sure but it sounded like Kira was making some reference to Lord Asano's wife.

Lord Asano, too, had trouble believing his ears as Kira spoke.

"You could have saved yourself all this trouble, you know," he said insinuatingly. "If your money means so much to you, there are other ways to satisfy my taste for delicacies. I hear you have a pretty wife with a round moonlike face..."

Lord Asano could take no more. The blood drained from his face and pounded in his chest, and his sword arm jerked to the hilt of his weapon. Kira's hand went instinctively to his own sword, although he had no intention of drawing it, but this was a tragic mistake. Lord Asano saw the move as an acceptance of his challenge and his sword blade flashed naked as he raised it high and slashed down in blind fury. Kira, struck high on the shoulder, stumbled and fell. Lord Asano raised his arm to strike again but Lord Daté and some of the others rushed forward to seize him. There was a second's stillness, broken only when Kajikawa gulped loudly and hurried away into the inner room.

Lord Asano went slack with a shudder as he looked down at the still figure of Kira and then at the men who took both his swords from him. He was still standing motionless, a glazed look in his eyes, when the sliding doors opened again and the Shogun Tsunayoshi himself stepped into the room. Behind him could be seen a group of boys in dance costume, all strangely silent and grotesquely frozen in position.

Tsunayoshi, more feminine appearing than ever in his dance costume, was not prepared for the sight which greeted him. He caught his breath sharply, then staggered back as though he might fall. Some of those present could guess what was going through his mind.

It was just seventeen years ago that a similar incident had taken place in this very room, and during all these years Tsunayoshi had been haunted by it. It had been his own prime minister who had been struck down at that time, instantly killed by a junior member of the court, who, it was said, resented the prime minister's taking over too many powers that rightly belonged to the Shogun. It was also said, behind closed doors, that Tsunayoshi himself was responsible for the attack, although this was never proved. The assassin was executed on the spot by the assembled lords, and his motives remained a secret.

Now it was as though the whole scene was being played out again before his eyes and he was plainly unnerved by the sight. A sudden rage took hold of him and the blood rushed to his face as he stamped forward to stand by Kira's motionless body. With a grimace of distaste, the Shogun ordered two servants to carry his no longer impeccable Master of Ceremonies into an anteroom, then turned to the others.

"What's happened here?" he demanded to know, but there was no immediate reply. "You, there," he said to Lord Daté. "Tell me what happened."

Daté released Lord Asano's arm and bowed, swallowing hard as he did so. Then he straightened and spoke briefly and formally, as though reporting to a superior on the field of battle.

"Lord Asano evidently took offense at something Lord Kira said. We saw that he was shocked. We saw that he drew his sword and struck Lord Kira. It was as though something beyond him was forcing..."

"He drew his sword and struck Kira?" interrupted the Shogun. "Does anyone know what Kira said to him to cause him to behave in such a lawless manner?"

No one answered, least of all Kajikawa, who was peeking through the sliding doors to the inner room and who knew when to keep his mouth shut.

"Very well, then, hold him here," said Tsunayoshi icily. He turned to Lord Asano. "You have no regard, sir, for the propriety of this court?"

"I'm sorry," said Lord Asano as he knelt and bowed his head to the floor. "I have no excuse."

"There are rules for every occasion," Tsunayoshi went on, "carefully thought out rules which everyone must obey. I make no exceptions in this regard—not even of my own kinsmen. Ignorance of the rules might make some difference, but I'm sure that you, sir, after so many years as a daimyo cannot claim such an exemption."

"No...no," murmured Lord Asano, feeling sure he must be having a bad dream from which he would soon wake.

Tsunayoshi turned to the others. "The crime is clear enough. So is the penalty. You will please keep this man in custody while I confer with my councilors. In the meantime the ceremony will have to be delayed."

He made an expression of distaste at the bloodstains on the floor, then turned away and started to go back through the sliding doors to the large hall beyond. One of his retinue of courtiers appeared in the doorway, but stepped back obsequiously to make way for the Shogun.

"It's terrible," said the Shogun to the courtier. "All our plans upset because of one irresponsible samurai who never learned how to behave in the castle. It may even mean canceling our dance performance."

Then they were gone and Lord Asano was left alone with his captors. He continued to kneel and look steadfastly at the floor while the rest of those present watched him in awed silence. His face maintained a stony calm, but inside his stomach was churning so that it was difficult to think straight. He felt close to being sick but took a firmer grip on himself, resolving to show nothing of weakness. His only thought was that he must prove to all that he did know his place.

An hour passed in silence before the sound of marching men was heard from outside. Lord Tamura, the red-faced and bustling Daimyo of Ichinoseki, burst in a side entrance with a squad of samurai and then stood indecisively when he saw Lord Asano's rigid pose. Lord Tamura had been a former high constable, which was presumably why Tsunayoshi had summoned him, but in this assignment he felt at a loss. It was easy to be commanding when dealing with the thieves and pickpockets of Edo, but to arrest a fellow daimyo was something else again. He approached the kneeling man with reluctance and placed his hand on his shoulder.

"By our Shogun's order," he said, and Lord Asano obediently got up to follow him out. There was a palanquin waiting outside along with a dozen samurai and more than thirty servants, but none of the faces were familiar and he looked around in vain for Kataoka. He was about to step into the palanquin when he was stopped by a word from Tamura who, in some embarrassment, handed him a cheap servant's dress and asked him to put it on over his court robes. Lord Asano was astounded by this effrontery until he realized that it was for his own benefit. In this garb he would not be recognized as he rode through the streets of Edo and would be spared public humiliation. With an expression of distaste he put it on and got in the palanquin, after which Lord Tamura had a large net thrown over it and the whole rig tied around with rope so there could be no chance of his prisoner escaping and bringing disgrace on his keeper. Then the order was given to move out and the procession set off for Lord Tamura's mansion. As they rounded the corner at the guard shack they passed close by the waiting Kataoka, who knew nothing of what had happened in the castle and had no idea that it was Lord Asano who passed by him as a prisoner.

It was afternoon before Kataoka really began to worry about his master. The ceremonies appeared to be over and the various lords summoned their palanquins and departed, but there was still no sign of Lord Asano. Finally he recognized Lord Daté's palanquin and hurried forward to intercept him.

Lord Daté was still stunned by the events of the morning and for a moment did not understand Kataoka's polite question. As to what had happened to Lord Asano he had no clear idea himself except that he had been taken away by Lord Tamura. Then he realized that Kataoka knew nothing of the attack on Kira, and tried to think of some diplomatic way of telling him and in effect breaking the news to all of Lord Asano's followers and family.

"Your master is at Lord Tamura's. I suggest you go there immediately."

"Is something wrong?" asked Kataoka in sudden alarm.

"There was an accident...Lord Kira and your master were involved..."

There was a short silence while Kataoka digested what he had been told. When he understood all the implications he felt a sinking feeling in the pit of his stomach and his mouth grew dry.

"Then there is no need for the palanquin to wait?" he stammered.

Lord Daté shook his head, then paused for a moment to see that Kataoka was capable of taking some positive action before he moved on. After all, it was the least he could do for a fellow daimyo.

With a quick bow of thanks Kataoka moved away. He did not dare to break the prohibition against running within the castle grounds but he reached Lord Asano's palanquin within the least possible time. Although his brain was whirling he composed a brief message for the bearers to take back to Hara. The men were from Ako and could be trusted, but still they were of lowly rank and did not have to know all the facts. He told their leader only that Lord Asano had decided to visit Lord Tamura and had gone to his mansion by other means. They were to return to their own quarters and give Hara the message that he was to join Kataoka at Tamura's immediately. Then he walked briskly beside them out of the castle grounds, back over the bridge across the moat and into the city streets. Now he could set his own pace and he ran as though devils were pursuing him in spite of the crush of the crowd. How could such a thing happen, his mind kept screaming, how could such a thing happen to his beloved master?...

At Tamura's mansion, Lord Asano was treated with politeness and even allowed to borrow a simple robe from his captor to replace his ludicrously out-of-place ceremonial trousers and *kamishimo*. Those present did not attempt to talk to him, being understandably unsure of his status, and he was put in a small, white-walled anteroom and allowed paper and brush to write a note to his wife. With an effort he managed to collect his thoughts and had begun a brief account of what had happened, stressing the inevitability of his showdown with Kira, when he was interrupted by the sounds of the arrival of one of the censors of Edo and two assistants. As official instruments of the Shogun's Council they had brought its sentence and Lord Asano heard them whisper it to Lord Tamura in the next room. He knew by Lord Tamura's shocked reaction that the sentence was a harsh one and that could mean only one thing—death! The rest of their whispers meant little to him: "...councilors opposed...Tsunayoshi adamant...his own chief councilor was struck down in similar fashion some years ago...an example must be made...."

Lord Tamura then came respectfully into the room and bowed low. "Our merciful Shogun has decreed that your execution should be swift and you should therefore be grateful to him. You have also been granted the privilege of dying in an honorable manner because of your rank," he said. Lord Asano remained silent and Tamura regarded his stoical acceptance of the verdict with approval. Then he added the final part of the sentence: "All property held in your name will be confiscated and placed under the protection of the Shogun's government until further notice."

In his mind Lord Asano heard the howling of the dogs again and felt the helpless sinking he had known in his dream, but he only stared at the blank white wall in front of him until Lord Tamura bowed and withdrew. After a moment Lord Asano bent forward to continue his letter but he was still not finished when Lord Tamura came back with the censor and his assistants. They waited for him to conclude his message and for the note to dry and be sealed. Then the censor stepped forward and started to help him rise. With dignity and authority Lord Asano shook off his arm and stood unaided. He had already started to follow Lord Tamura out into the garden when there was a commotion in the entry way. Kataoka had arrived and breathlessly asked to be allowed to see his master. Lord Tamura conferred briefly with the censor and the request was granted, although they stood close by, anxious to conclude matters as swiftly as possible. Kataoka hesitated before the others, but could not control his emotions and burst forth in a heartfelt apology for not having been aware of the terrible events in the castle. Lord Asano raised his hand.

"I'm glad to see you, Gengoemon," he said, calling him by his given name. "Yours is the first friendly face I've seen since morning."

Kataoka felt the tears well into his eyes but Lord Asano pretended not to notice. He handed his follower the note.

"This is my farewell to the others. Please deliver it to...to my wife." He paused for a moment and a faraway look came into his eyes. "Tell everyone...tell them...Oishi will know what to do."

In the garden, before Lord Tamura's entire company of samurai, three mats had been placed on the ground and covered with a white rug. In the early evening it was beginning to grow dark and paper lanterns were lit at each corner of the improvised stage. Lord Asano was led to seat himself in the center of the rug before a small stand on which lay a dirk with a nine-inch blade. Lord Asano picked it up to look at it curiously and saw that it was an heirloom of the Tamura family. He gave Lord Tamura a quick smile of appreciation and then listened without expression as the censor officially read the terms of the offense and the sentence. The dogs were howling in his head again and he felt rather than heard when the reading was finished. He knew what was expected of him and he had confidence in his ability to perform with the dignity required. At least when it came to this, no one would be able to say he did not know his place.

He grasped the dirk in both hands and murmured a quick prayer as he placed it low on the left side of his abdomen. He plunged it in and drew it across, and then all sound stopped as one of the assistant censors stepped forward to behead him with one powerful swing of his long sword.

Chapter Three

"WHY AREN'T YOU WITH OUR MASTER?" was
Oishi's first angry response when the dirty, sweat-covered
Hara was brought before him in the middle of the night. In
the old warrior's present condition he was a disgrace to the
rank of samurai, and Oishi suffered the shame he knew Lord
Asano would feel to see one of his men like this. But at Hara's
first wild-eyed cry, when the servant who had brought him
was gone, such trivial considerations were forgotten.

"Our master is dead," Hara blurted out, "and the castle is to
be confiscated!"

Oishi felt as though water had been poured into his ears
while he was asleep. He was stunned, speechless, sure that he
must still be asleep and dreaming the most horrible dream
imaginable. He wanted to call out to Hara to say no more, but
he forced himself to listen, incredible as it all seemed. Lord
Asano had been like his brother; his loss was insupportable.

Hara, kneeling on the floor of the anteroom, rocked his
head alternately down and up again as he sobbed out his story
while the ungainly Mimura, who had accompanied him, nodded tearfully.

"It was Kira who did it! Kira, the court Master of Ceremonies, who provoked our master into an attack in the castle. Our master was forced to draw his sword and strike him down, even though he knew as we all do the penalty for drawing one's sword in the castle of the Shogun!"

"And the sentence was carried out so soon?" Oishi cried, even as he took a silent oath of vengeance against those responsible.

"The same day," Hara said hopelessly. "Before we even knew what was happening."

"What about Lady Asano?" Oishi asked quickly. "Do you know what's happened to her?"

"Gone," said Hara with a sob. "As soon as our Lord was dead, the soldiers of the court came to the mansion and confiscated everything. All of us were turned out and Lady Asano was sent back to her parents' home. She is not to return to Ako or attempt to contact any member of the family on pain of death."

Oishi felt a stab at his heart as he thought of the little girl asleep in a nearby room, waiting trustfully for her mother and father. Suddenly he was overwhelmed by the enormity of the tragedy that had struck at the house of Asano and all its members. He turned to Mimura and sent him to fetch old Chuzaemon Yoshida, one of the elder samurai of Ako whose counsel would be welcome.

"How did you learn all this?" Oishi asked Hara, who was now beginning to show extreme fatigue after his arduous journey.

"Kataoka was there when our master committed seppuku at Lord Tamura's—at least he was permitted that kind of death. The rest of us were too late. The palanquin bearers were delayed in the crowded streets and when we got the message, we went there but it was all over. We then hurried back to our own mansion to protect our mistress, but the Shogun's forces arrived with the official order and at her command we obeyed it. There was nothing we could save. The order read 'immediate confiscation of all property' and it was carried out to the letter."

"And the castle here in Ako is to be confiscated, too?"

"Yes," said Hara in a barely audible tone. "A force will be arriving from Edo to carry out those instructions."

"And what of the men you left behind in Edo? Are they on their way back? We should not be divided at a time like this."

Hara looked up at him and explained. "I left young Horibe in charge. He and the others are closing out our Edo accounts as I thought you would wish them to. They are also watching to see when the enemy—I mean the Shogun's troops—leave Edo."

Oishi looked at him sharply. Hara's attitude was not hard to fathom. He meant they should prepare to stand a siege of the castle and go down fighting. And Hara might be right—at least it was a positive plan of action to redeem their lost honor— but still Oishi felt he should not make any such weighty decisions before he was in full possession of all the facts.

They were interrupted by the arrival of the gray-haired old Yoshida, whose Buddha-like face was, for once, wrinkled in concern. They told him what had happened and he crumpled to the floor, trying to control his cries of lamentation. In his whole lifetime as a samurai, he had never known a moment so agonizing. Oishi felt his own stomach knot in despair and frustration but he refused to give way to an emotional outbreak. He was in charge, the others looked to him as an example, and he must remain coldly in charge of himself if his decisions were to have the merit of his best thinking.

To give the old man time to recover himself, Oishi asked Mimura to bring a *hibachi* without disturbing any of the other servants. For the time being, until they decided on a course of action, it would be better if no one else knew what terrible problems they faced. Mimura had been in the Asanos' service since childhood and could be trusted to say nothing.

When the charcoal-burning *hibachi* was brought, Oishi directed that it be placed by Yoshida, who now sat with tears streaming down his cheeks. Oishi and Hara sat close to him for warmth while Mimura folded his long legs under him and sat by the door as a guard against eavesdroppers.

"Perhaps we should call Ono," Yoshida suggested uncertainly. As treasurer of the clan, Ono had considerable say in fiscal matters, but at the moment Oishi did not think his advice would count for much. Ono would be inclined to put matters of justice and honor below those of finances and Oishi was in no mood for quibbling.

"The matter does not concern Ono," he told Yoshida. "We can decide what must be done among ourselves."

Oishi glanced at Hara as he finished speaking and saw the big man nod vigorously. He had no more use for Ono than his leader did.

There was silence for a while as each sat busy with his own thoughts. To dull his bitter sense of loss, Oishi deliberately turned his mind to the past, to memories of the instructions he had received as a young samurai. His lessons had been given in this very room and he could hear old Yamaga Soko's warnings that the times were getting soft and that the strict observance of Confucian ethics was being undermined by the preachers of "new Confucianism" who were beginning to infest the court. That was why Yamaga had been exiled to the countryside—because he was out of step with the times—but he found willing listeners in the samurai of Ako, who were far removed from the softness and politics of the court. Oishi heard his condemnation of the Edo court again as though they were being spoken at this moment: "The sacrifice of the noble to the elegant." And that had turned out to be a prophecy of Lord Asano's death.

He thought of the circumstances of his master's attack on Kira. He had no doubt it was justified, but if only it had taken place somewhere else!

It was not his place to criticize the Shogun, no matter what the circumstances, but it was disturbing to consider how inconsistent their ruler was in his observation of the teachings of Buddha. True, a Buddha-like detestation of violence and cruelty was at the core of his Life Preservation Laws, but had they been applied equally to the life of Lord Asano? And what of the vanity of wealth and power, the duty of abstinence from the grosser pleasures, the beauty of the life of seclusion and pious meditation? No, Tsunayoshi took from Buddhism only what suited his own purposes and this left his policies open to question by anyone bold enough to do so.

Oishi raised his eyes from the pictures he had been seeing in the glowing coals of the *hibachi* and saw that old Yoshida was watching him. No doubt he had been thinking the same thoughts and there was no need to say them aloud. Yoshida shivered and shook his head, then rubbed his hand over his close-cropped hair.

"We must make some sort of plan," he offered in a vague manner.

The words struck Oishi strangely. He had been counting strongly on the old man's advice but now he saw that there was little to hope for from this direction. Nothing like this had ever happened before in the history of the clan, and Yoshida was no more able to cope with it than the youngest samurai in the castle. Oishi would be glad to have the old man's counsel, but he knew that from now on all decisions must come from him as chief retainer. He had no fear of not being strong enough to make them and to see that they were carried out; he only hoped that his judgments would be carefully arrived at and truly best for the house of Asano and the spirit of his departed master.

Hara rubbed his hands together and restlessly changed his position. In his mind this meeting was a council of war and its object was to map a plan of defense for the castle.

"Shouldn't we summon all the men?" he growled.

Oishi hesitated and was glad when Yoshida cleared his throat as a signal that he would answer.

"Let's wait until daybreak," the old man said. "If our warriors are to be needed for any extraordinary purposes, even if it is only to receive the announcement of their master's death, it would be just as well to let them get all the rest they can beforehand."

"I agree with Yoshida-sensei," said Oishi, giving the old man the honorific title of "teacher" to lend his remarks more weight. "In the morning we will all be able to think more clearly and can face our new problems with more assurance."

"We should begin now to think of our defenses," Hara muttered doggedly, and Oishi, turning aside in annoyance, caught a troubled glance thrown at the grizzled old warrior by Mimura. He sensed that something about Hara's attitude was upsetting his servant, but he hesitated to ask for fear of embarrassing the clumsy young man. Instead he turned to Hara.

"Have you told me everything, Hara? Everything I need to know about this tragic affair? Kira was killed and our master was condemned to death and loss of property—is that the whole story?

Hara hesitated. "On one point there is some doubt...Kira was taken away in a hurry and it's possible he could have survived the attack, although it's not very likely. Otherwise I've told you all I know. I still don't see why you hesitate to plan the defense of the castle. The Shogun's troops will be arriving any day now and we must be ready to give a good account of ourselves."

"We'll be ready for whatever comes, don't worry. Now I think the best plan for all of us is to try to get some sleep. I must have more time to think before I can make any sort of worthwhile plans."

He rose and stretched, then bowed a polite goodnight to the bent form of Yoshida and nodded more casually in Hara's direction. As he left the room he was followed by Mimura, although there was no real reason for the servant to accompany him. He kept silent until they reached the door of his room, then turned to the gangling young man.

"Bathe yourself and get some rest," he told him. "Tomorrow will be a hard day for all of us. I appreciate all you have done and know that you always have the best welfare of the house of Asano at heart."

He half-turned to go but was stopped by Mimura's sudden action of dropping to his knees and touching his head to the floor.

"I must tell you," he said in a hoarse whisper. "I was forced by Hara to promise to say nothing, but I feel that would be unfair to you who carries the final responsibility!"

Oishi gently lifted the boy by the shoulder of his ragged cloak until they were standing eye to eye. He said nothing, waiting for the boy to resolve the conflict within him.

"Before we left Edo," Mimura finally blurted out, "we went to visit Daigaku Asano, our Lord's younger brother, and his uncle Lord Toda, the Daimyo of Ogaki. They were holding up under their sorrow as well as could be expected, although as you know Daigaku is a rather frail young man and Lord Toda is now quite old. They knew all that had happened. They knew about the order to surrender the castle at Ako to the Shogun's representatives."

"And?"

"And they advised Hara to tell you that we should surrender peaceably in order not to increase the disgrace that has already fallen on the family."

Oishi let go of the boy and nodded that he might go.

Mimura hurried away down the corridor, praying that he had done the right thing. Even so, Hara might kill him if he found out he had broken his promise.

Oishi had been given another unpleasant surprise and he appreciated more than ever the complexity of the problems he had to solve. He could not oppose the wishes of the family and yet he could see why a man of action like Hara would refuse to carry their message. When there were two valid viewpoints to reconcile, it was not always easy to choose the side that was right.

He went to his room and got a warm cloak. He had been profoundly shaken by the news about his master and he knew there was no use trying to sleep. There was only one place where he might get some help for the questions that were troubling him, and he quietly slipped outside the castle to go there. The guard on duty at the main gate let him out a small side door and politely concealed his surprise at such unusual actions on the part of his superior.

The night was dark with a cold breeze and Oishi shivered as he started to climb a small hill behind the castle. As he ascended, the wind grew stronger and he pulled his cloak more tightly around him. Looking back as he walked, he could see the dim outlines of the castle towers against the night sky; looking ahead he began to make out the shadows of a small cluster of gravestones on top of the hill. This was Kegaku-ji, the temple in Ako that constituted the Asano family burial grounds.

He made his way to the center of the tiny fenced area and looked around. Here were buried the ashes of all the members of the Asano family he had ever known and many that had died before he was born. He moved slowly around, reading the familiar inscriptions on the pointed stone markers, then paused to look upward at the sky.

"My Lord Asano," he said with great intensity, "I call to you in the spirit world."

There was no answer but the moan of the wind and the nervous friction of leafless branches, but still Oishi felt closer to his lord than he would anywhere else and took some comfort in being able to openly express his thoughts.

"If only I'd been with you," Oishi cried as he knelt with his hands pressed together and lifted upward in a gesture that asked for forgiveness. Then he dropped his hands to his knees and cast his eyes down in humility.

"Please know, my lord, that we attach no blame to your action. You did what any man would have done to protect his honor. The blame is all on the other side."

Oishi was thinking that he had known Lord Asano all his life and that in spite of his occasional outbursts of temper, there was no more worthy daimyo in all Japan. This section of the country was known for its strong adherence to the traditional virtues of the samurai and there was no one more generous, more brave, more earnest in trying to live up to those ideals than Lord Asano. Oishi would follow such a master anywhere, even to the grave if necessary, and he would have no hesitation in drawing his dirk and joining him at this very moment if he thought the gesture would accomplish anything.

His hand went to the blade of the knife at his belt but then dropped away. His primary duty now was to the living. To Lord Asano's widow and little daughter and to all the retainers and people in the castle town who would look to him for guidance. If the time came when his suicide would serve a purpose, he would be ready.

Now there were decisions to be made and he was depending on the spirit of Lord Asano to guide him in making the right ones. Would his master want him to peaceably give up the castle or would he want him to stand a siege, fighting to the last man? Or should they simply all kneel in front of the castle and commit seppuku together as a protest against an unfair sentence? Oishi was used to carrying out orders, not formulating policy, and this was a difficult experience for him.

He realized how much depended on his ability to decide what was best for all and the responsibility weighed on him heavily. Who could judge if his choices were the right ones? The silent voice of Lord Asano would guide him, but in the end he knew he must judge himself. The path of honor was easy to follow when it was easy to see. When there were conflicts between choice of action, such as Hara had raised, the solutions could not be expected to satisfy everyone.

In the deep woods, higher up the mountain, a fox barked at the wind and Oishi lifted his eyes. He saw the grave markers standing around him like an impenetrable fence and he imagined that this was how the spirit of Lord Asano saw them, too. His soul was in torment because of the dishonor his act had brought on Ako, and he would find true repose only when some resolution to the present state of affairs could be found. It was up to Oishi to find a way to bring this about.

He sighed, then rose to bow respectfully to all the tombs in the graveyard. He felt the coldness of dread in his bowels as he did so. The sudden extinction of this noble family was almost too awful a thought to bear. If they surrendered, these graves would be neglected and the spirits would search in vain for proper homage and care from their descendants. Those living would be denied the comforts of their ancestors' blessings and would wander the earth dispossessed of part of their souls. The urge to strike out against those who would bring this to pass came strongly over him, but he knew in his heart that a siege would be a futile gesture. In the end they would lose and the graves of the ancestors would be just as neglected.

Suddenly the immensity of what was going to happen to himself personally struck home for the first time. He would no longer be a respected samurai; he would be a ronin, a man without a master, one of those pitiful ones whose days of usefulness and glory were gone. He would be forced to become a soldier of fortune or drop out of the military ranks altogether. Either choice was a miserable one. Perhaps Hara was right and he should ignore the orders of Daigaku and Toda. It would be better to go down fighting than to watch his family starve and sink into the bottomless, honorless pit of poverty.

Then he shook his head free of such thoughts and went back down the hill to the castle to plan what he would say at the meeting that must be called. In the morning he would ask his wife to tell Lord Asano's little daughter that her father and mother would not be coming home.

Chapter Four

THE NEXT MORNING Oishi briefly told his wife what had happened in Edo. In the face of such a tragedy she was naturally shaken, but true to the samurai tradition to which she was born, she did not break down in useless tears. She was given her instructions about the little girl and bowed respectfully as she left to carry them out. The future of their own family was not discussed; there would be time for that later.

Weary from lack of sleep, Oishi moved slowly toward the front of the castle where the followers were to assemble, but as he passed the door of the room where he had met with Hara and Yoshida the night before, he heard voices and paused.

Someone was reading from the works of Confucius in a droning monotone and he could not resist the temptation to move silently to the sliding door and push it open a crack.

The scene inside was just as he had imagined and it took him back nearly thirty years to his own young manhood. His fifteen-year-old son Chikara, already nearly as big as a man, was kneeling on the *tatami* before a low writing table, patiently practicing the complicated brush strokes of Japanese character writing. Opposite him on a cushion, his pale-faced teacher in a priestly cap and flowing gray robes sat dictating from the works of Confucius. Oishi knew that through this constant exposure to literary culture and moral teachings, the boy would soon be as thoroughly indoctrinated as he himself was in the wisdom of the past.

Although the barren room was wide and light it was separated from the garden beyond by only a partition of paper *shoji* and was bitterly cold. Chikara had evidently been sitting stock still for several hours and Oishi noted with pride that although his hands were red with cold, he made no attempt to warm them or to shift his position. His son was following admirably in his own footsteps, and he reflected that the boy would soon be a man with a man's responsibilities. In view of present events, he would finish his apprenticeship none too soon.

Quietly, Oishi closed the door and went on down the corridor until the teacher's voice faded away. When he reached the front door of the castle it was opened for him by a guard and he took a deep breath as he stepped outside into the cold sunlight to face the assembled men.

All the Asano retainers of samurai rank had been summoned to the meeting. Ordinarily they would have formed in ranks outside the wall, but in the interests of privacy Oishi had summoned them to the front steps of the castle proper and here they gathered, under its soaring towers, over three hundred fighting men surrounding the entrance and overflowing into the paths of the garden beyond.

In attire they were all alike; semibattle dress, ready to don their armor if it should be necessary. In age they varied widely; from men in their sixties who might be more of a hindrance than a help on the battlefield to boys in their teens who had strength and agility but lacked wisdom and experience. The majority were in their thirties and forties, seasoned in life and combat, and it was to these that Oishi primarily addressed himself.

In spite of all precautions, rumors had begun to circulate. The precipitate and unexplained arrival of Hara and Mimura in the middle of the night could not help but be noticed and commented on. Conjectures of all kinds passed among them while they waited, but their murmurs were quickly stilled when Oishi raised his hand for silence.

In the chill morning air, the frost on his breath was appropriate to his cold words: "Our master is dead." They stared at him in disbelief. Had he shouted it with his sword flung high they would have understood that it was a call to action, but the tone in which he pronounced the words told them the situation was hopeless and that there was nothing to be done. As he went on to explain what had happened, there were tears of sorrow and of anger that came to the eyes of many who had never wept before in their lives.

He told them how the Shogun's Master of Ceremonies had goaded their master beyond endurance, and there were angry mutterings among them. He told them that Lady Asano was in exile and that the Shogun's representatives were coming to take over the castle and all the lands at Ako. There were again murmurs of outrage but they stopped when Oishi concluded, without even a glance in Hara's direction, that it was the decision of Daigaku Asano, the heir to the title, that they relinquish the castle peaceably.

Hara looked up quickly at this, then narrowed his eyes as they sought out Mimura. Being only a servant, he was not present at the meeting, but Hara vowed he would make him regret his betrayal when he found him. He had not long to wait for his man. Mimura unexpectedly appeared before them in the doorway to the castle and Oishi broke off to see what emergency had brought him there.

When he had been officially recognized, Mimura hurried to Oishi's side and all present turned their eyes on him as he whispered something into their leader's ear. Oishi looked startled, then nodded and the servant withdrew. Oishi turned to the assembled men.

"A messenger has arrived from Edo," he told them. "Gengoemon Kataoka has brought fresh news from the capital."

Kataoka, his monkey face grim and his clothes in tatters, hobbled out on sore legs and bowed deeply to Oishi. He was obviously exhausted and had trouble breathing but did his utmost to hold himself at rigid attention while he was the focal point of the eyes of all of his comrades.

"Please," Oishi said, "tell us what you have learned. You may speak to the whole group together. We are all equally involved in this matter."

Kataoka hesitated, glanced around to identify some of the faces nearest him, then shouted the fateful words:

"Kira lives!"

Instantly the whole tenor of the meeting changed. Sorrow and hopelessness changed to pure rage and Hara was the first to voice it.

"Then he must die!" he cried, and there was a tremendous answering shout from the assembly. A surge of passion rose within Oishi, too, but he deliberately forced it down and waited for the uproar to subside. When the men saw that he wished to speak they gradually quieted down, although there were puzzled murmurings about his strangely cold response to the news that their dead master's arch-enemy still lived.

"I agree that Kira should die," he said finally. "There's nothing I'd like more than to launch an assault on him this very minute. But..." and he paused as his jaw tightened, "...we should not be hasty in rushing into action. I hardly think that this group is sufficient in size or armament to undertake a punitive expedition to Edo to attack someone behind the walls of the Shogun's castle. We'll leave such discussions until later. At this meeting we are only concerned with the coming surrender of the castle and I have certain recommendations to make in this regard."

This was more than some of the men could take. Their mutterings sounded mutinously in Oishi's ears but only Hara was bold enough to stand and speak. He addressed his leader formally, but with an undertone of incredulity in his voice.

"Please, Oishi-dono, I don't think I understand you correctly. We have just been told that our lord's enemy, the one who caused his death, still lives, and you say there are more important things to discuss?"

He looked to the crowd for approval and received it in their shouts. Bolder now, he continued to lay it on the line. "Does not even the peaceful Confucius say that no man may live under the same sky with the murderer of his lord?"

The men shouted again in agreement until Oishi held up his hand in a commanding gesture.

"You forget yourselves," he said. "Your loyalty is to the house of Asano. Our first duty is to follow the command of our lord's brother and the rightful heir to this fief." He paused to look directly at Hara. "Does not Confucius also say that of the five virtues, loyalty dwarfs all other moral obligations?"

"Our lord's brother is not our lord!" came a shout from the rear and there were answering murmurs of assent. Hara excitedly took the floor again and addressed Oishi directly.

"There is no question of loyalty," he said. "We're all loyal. The only question is how we can best show that loyalty. And I say that if we *don't* take revenge on Kira, we're bound to appear as cowards and weaklings in the eyes of our countrymen!"

Oishi answered him icily. "And I say it doesn't matter what anyone thinks as long as we're convinced in our own minds that we're right. Think for a moment of our mistress, Lady Asano, and of her little daughter. Will taking the life of a miserable creature like Kira help regain their home? More likely they would only be executed along with the rest of us for our unsuccessful attempt. Consider also what such open rebellion would mean to Ako. Will the ancestors of the Asano family be pleased to have their tombs desecrated in view of a ruined castle?"

"Will those ancestors sleep peacefully in death knowing that Lord Asano's followers were too cowardly to avenge his death?" shouted back Hara. There was a cry of agreement from many of the men and Oishi hesitated, then quietly signaled to Yoshida in the crowd. The gray-haired old man stood and made his way to the front of the group.

"I must reprimand you, Soemon Hara," he said sternly, "for what you have just said to our leader. There is no reason to impugn his loyalty, just because he doesn't agree with you on the best way to show it. For my part, I find his position entirely reasonable. By showing no resistance and obeying the Shogun's commands to the best of our ability we will gain more toward what we want than by seeking a blood bath. If we remain blameless, the Shogun may in time see where the true blame lies and punish Kira himself."

"'He may in time?'" mocked Hara. "You're an old man, Yoshida. Don't you want to see justice done before you die?"

"I am an old man," agreed Yoshida. "And more than anything before I die, I want to see this house restored. I say we should appeal the Shogun's decision before taking any other action."

There was a murmur of approval to this course of action, which Oishi was relieved to hear. At least they were not *all* against him. There was a possibility now that he could reach a compromise that would satisfy both factions, at least for the time being. He was pleased with himself for having arranged beforehand that Yoshida should propose this plan so that he himself would appear more in the light of an impartial judge.

Ono, the treasurer, now stood and for a moment Oishi regretted he had not consulted with him beforehand.

Ono was an elderly man with a studious look, a tight smile, and a mind that clicked away at a problem like the counters on his abacus. His opinions carried considerable weight and he was capable of making trouble, but as Oishi had anticipated he was in accord with Yoshida's plan. He, too, was for waiting till the last possible moment to make a decision.

"I agree with both speakers that we should make an appeal," Oishi told the group when Ono was through. "It is in no way contrary to the wishes of Daigaku Asano—from what I have been able to learn of his views." He looked directly at Hara who squirmed uncomfortably. "And besides, such a course has the advantage of buying us time to prepare."

"Prepare for what?" asked Hara.

"For a siege, if our petition is denied," Oishi answered. This was the first time he had hinted at positive action and he could tell by the sharp intakes of breaths around him that it came as a not unwelcome prospect. "I will write the petition myself today and send it by courier to the proper officials in Edo. In the meantime I ask all of you to search your souls to decide the best course of action for yourselves. So much has happened so quickly that I recommend you all take time to think. We will meet tomorrow morning to discuss measures of resistance, if it becomes necessary to offer it, and I suggest that only those prepared to fight to the death attend."

A hush fell over the group and Oishi spoke more slowly so that there could be no mistake about what he was saying. "We can fight, we can die, or we may decide, if we are too few in number, that it might be better to simply kneel in front of the castle and commit seppuku as a greeting to the Shogun's representatives—if that doesn't seem like too cowardly a gesture."

There was complete silence now, even on Hara's part. Seppuku was their last great resource for combating injustice. It was part of the training of a samurai that he would know how and when to take this ultimate step, yet this was the first time any of them had had it offered as a practical alternative. Oishi had indeed given them much to think about.

When the meeting was adjourned and the men returned to their duties, Oishi turned to the waiting Kataoka to question him closely about how things were going in Edo.

"Fine—fine," Kataoka nodded briskly, in spite of his weariness. "Young Horibe is doing a good job."

He went on to tell how Horibe was keeping close watch on the exit routes from the city so that he would know when the troops were being sent to take over the castle at Ako. He was also keeping track of Kira's movements so that he would know when the moment had arrived to strike. Oishi was concerned that Horibe, who had a reputation for being hotheaded, might take too much into his own hands, but Kataoka assured him that all those in Edo were pledged to follow the orders of their leader in Ako. Relieved to hear this, Oishi sent the exhausted man for food and rest, and started to walk toward the stable area. On the way he was joined by Hara, who was full of apologies.

"Please believe that I'm sorry if I said anything to offend you," he said. "I just can't help myself when I get excited. I know it gets me into nothing but trouble, but I've always been like this and I can't seem to stop."

Oishi smiled. "I know you well enough to realize that," he said. "And don't you worry about what happened in the meeting. You represent one viewpoint and I'm glad you do it so forcefully. We're asking these men to consider pledging their lives to our decision and they should have a clear-cut choice offered to them. We must also take care that those who depart from the way of the sword do not lose face with their comrades."

Hara looked at him with respect. His own mind was incapable of seeing into the situation so deeply and he was impressed by a leader who had both brains and a fighting heart.

"It must be hard for you," he said humbly, "to have to consider the views of all...You know you can always rely on me to carry out your orders."

Oishi smiled at him. "Thank you, old friend. I know I can count on you in any crisis."

Hara bowed his head in gratitude and together they walked on. When they reached the stables, Oishi took a moment to inspect the rows of stalls where the few remaining horses stood unbrushed and with tangled manes. He shook his head in dismay at their condition, then called for the head groom. When the man appeared, as shabby looking as his charges, Oishi unexpectedly gave orders that the horses were to be combed and their hooves pared so that they would appear at their best. The groom was amazed at his words and happily hurried away before Oishi could change his mind. Hara's mouth, too, had fallen open at the command.

"Then you are going to fight?" he asked uncertainly.

"Not necessarily," said Oishi. "But even if we decide to evacuate the castle peaceably, it wouldn't do to post our last guard on shabby mounts, would it?"

Hara could not help but agree and turned to watch the groom as he briskly started to work. Then he realized that Oishi was staring at him and he faced his leader somewhat uneasily.

"I've forgiven you for your remarks at the meeting," Oishi said, "but I cannot so easily excuse you for not telling me about your meeting with Daigaku and Lord Toda before you returned to Ako. Without that information I might have made a blunder that could have cost us all our lives for nothing."

"I'm sorry," murmured Hara.

"I might be more inclined to forgive you, however, if you promise you'll do nothing to harm Mimura for his brave act."

Hara grimaced, then nodded reluctantly. He had been looking forward to the pleasure of beating the talkative servant to within an inch of his life.

"Keep that promise," Oishi said gravely, "or I will let everyone know that you tried to deceive me."

His manner told Hara that this was no idle threat, and the old warrior bowed thoughtfully as Oishi walked away. Then he scratched his head and sighed.

Now Oishi faced the first real test of his leadership. If too few appeared at the second meeting, all hope of revenge would be lost. At the appointed hour, he watched from inside the castle door as the samurai assembled. He was intent on counting them when he was startled by the arrival of someone at his side. It was Hara, also anxious to see who was with them and who was not. As they counted together it was soon apparent that the turnout would be much smaller than the day before; when the time came for the meeting to begin there were only sixty or so present out of the original three hundred.

Hara was bitterly disappointed but Oishi took this development more philosophically.

"At least now we know who we can depend on," he told Hara with a wry smile.

"But what about the siege?" Hara asked anxiously. "You said that would be our next step if the petition was denied, didn't you?"

Oishi pointed to the group outside. "There can be no siege. Not with those few men at our disposal. And if you look closely you'll see that many of them are either too young or too old to put up a good fight."

Hara shook his head. "Then we have no choice but to surrender and give up everything without a struggle."

Oishi smiled, but it was not a pleasant smile. "Oh, we still have a choice to make." Then he stepped out before the assembly and raised his arm for silence. In his hand he held two documents.

"I have here a petition to the Shogun's representatives requesting leniency for the survivors of the Asano clan—that they be allowed to keep their land and other possessions because of their long and illustrious history of service to the Shogun and his ancestors before him. It is merely a polite request for restitution on behalf of Lady Asano and Daigaku Asano and whatever its effect I don't think it can do any harm. I am asking Gengoemon Kataoka to deliver it, in spite of his recent hard journey, because he is familiar with Edo and because he has a certain ability to think quickly and to make the best of any bargain that might be offered."

Kataoka rose from his cross-legged position in front of the gathering and came to take the document with a respectful bow. Then he sat down again as Oishi continued.

"Now, if the petition is accepted, we have nothing more to worry about. If, on the other hand, it is rejected, we must make a choice regarding our course of action. As I see it, we have but two alternatives: either to kneel before the castle and commit seppuku as a final protest, or to surrender the castle peaceably...and then split up and wait until the right moment to take revenge on Kira himself!"

Hara was the first to his feet with a cheer for the latter course and the others were not far behind him. Oishi smiled briefly at their enthusiasm, but then raised his hand again with a more serious expression.

"I must make sure you realize that however appealing such a course may appear to men of action like you, it is still against the law to take revenge. So it would be well to keep in mind that even if we are successful we will be guilty of an illegal act. I need hardly add that the punishment is death. Let no one have any illusions about that. Whether we commit seppuku by our own hands or are crucified by the executioner, our ultimate end is to die. This is a band of death, but death with honor!"

The cheering was not as robust now, but it rang with sincerity and Oishi was satisfied that those present could be depended on to stand and fight to the end. Now he unrolled his second document and laid it flat on the steps of the castle. It was a solemn pledge of loyalty and he asked them all to step forward and sign. As the men gathered eagerly around, Oishi noticed that one boy among them appeared to be barely in his teens, and he stopped him to question him about his age. The boy swore he was sixteen, however, and his manner was so stalwart that Oishi did not have the heart to challenge him further. He was allowed to sign, as were all the others present.

When it came to Hara's turn, he made a gesture with the writing brush toward the door of the castle and Oishi turned to see to what he was pointing. The door was slightly ajar and Oishi could see enough of the man standing inside to recognize him as Mimura. At first he was angry that a servant should be so bold as to eavesdrop on their meeting, but then he got the full import of Hara's signal.

"Mimura," he called, and the man stepped awkwardly out into the sunlight. Oishi turned to the group. "Here is another who would join our forces. Even though he is only of servant rank, I for one have no objection to his becoming our comrade in arms. He has demonstrated that he is as loyal as any of us. What do you say?"

There was a general murmur of approval, led by Hara, and the overjoyed Mimura was allowed to sign. His was the sixty-second signature and with it Oishi's band of vengeance was formed.

Chapter Five

AFTER KATAOKA HAD LEFT FOR EDO, Oishi and his men turned their attention to bringing the castle and the surrounding land into first-class condition. If they waited until the petition was officially denied, and they had to admit to themselves that this was a definite possibility, there would not be time to put things in order before the Shogun's representatives arrived.

Work was begun on minor repairs to the castle itself and a complete inventory made of all property. Ono, as treasurer, was given the responsibility of bringing accounts up to date and collecting all currency in circulation. This would not be surrendered to the Shogun, but distributed among members of the clan at the proper time as Oishi saw fit.

On horseback, Oishi toured the area, trying to anticipate any discrepancies the Shogun's representatives might notice. He found stone bridges that were crumbling away, wooden fences with broken boards, thatched roofs that needed repairing, small roadside temples and shrines that had become shabby looking, and a certain carelessness in town about keeping filth out of the streets. When he saw one peasant woman hold her child over an open gutter, he called to her to use a bucket instead. In this instance he was concerned not only about appearances but also with the practical aspects of using the material in the fields as fertilizer.

Everyone was set to work. On the biggest job of all, the repair of the main road from the town to the castle, even the samurai pitched in beside the farmers and townspeople to get the job done. This project entailed hauling large quantities of rocks from nearby stream beds and long bucket brigades were quickly set up. Soon hundreds of laborers were lined up along the road, toiling in the chill sunlight from dawn till dusk, often with frost on their breaths as well as perspiration on their bodies.

Oishi was checking the progress on the road one morning in late March when Kataoka arrived back in Ako, breathless and dirty. The dust was caked in the wrinkles of his face and his eyes were tiny red slits in the grime as he tumbled off his horse almost at Oishi's feet.

"I am sorry," he said, bowing his head into the dusty road. "Somehow, along the route, I missed the Shogun's representatives. They had already left Edo when I got there."

For a moment Oishi felt a twinge of despair. His first thought was of Lord Asano's little daughter. He did not know what instructions the Shogun might have given in her case. Her mother had been forbidden to see any member of the clan, but did this apply to her own daughter? He realized that time was running out and questioned Kataoka abruptly.

"Why didn't Horibe send word? He was supposed to be watching the exits to the city, wasn't he?"

"They left by a roundabout way," Kataoka answered. "You should know that popular feeling in Edo is against Kira, and the Shogun evidently thought it best to keep the departure of his troops a secret."

Oishi was both surprised and pleased to hear that public opinion was with them, but that did not alter the fact that officials were on their way to confiscate the castle.

"Do you have any idea when they will reach Ako?"

"Within two or three days," was Kataoka's best estimate.

Oishi quickly began to revise in his mind his plans for additional renovation of the castle, but his thoughts were interrupted by Kataoka's next remark.

"I hope I didn't exceed my authority, Oishi-dono, but when I found I was too late I went to see Daigaku Asano at his uncle's house. I thought they might have some instructions about the petition."

"Yes?" said Oishi, with a flash of interest.

"They read the petition and seemed quite upset by it. They said that under no circumstances must you resist the confiscation of the castle. And they sent you this letter." He took it out of his breastplate and handed it over with an apologetic bow.

Oishi took it and opened it to read. Daigaku and Toda both felt that the idea of a petition was a good one and that most of his requests seemed reasonable enough—although they had some objections to Oishi's reference to the difficulty he was having controlling his men, which could be interpreted as a threat—but they insisted that the castle be given up peaceably even if the petition were refused.

Oishi smiled. He was not surprised at the letter's contents and Kataoka was relieved to see that he was not to be reprimanded for his actions. There was one more piece of information Oishi wanted very much to know, but he deliberately put his question in an offhand, casual manner.

"And what of Lord Kira? He's recovering from his wound, I imagine?"

Kataoka looked at him quickly. He knew Oishi too well to think that any of his questions were idle.

"Horibe reports that he is well on the road to recovery. We have a man posted day and night near the entrance to the castle and when Kira is able to travel we will be informed."

Oishi's jaw set more firmly as he visualized Kira alive and well and behaving as though nothing had happened. A flash of fury went through him but he resolutely put it down. There would be time for Kira later. As long as he stayed within the Shogun's castle there was nothing they could do.

Later, in the same lesson room where he had received Hara on that black night when their world began to crumble, Oishi went over the situation with Yoshida. He told the old man it relieved his mind to have written authority to give up the castle to the Shogun's men, but he was concerned about Daigaku and his uncle's attitude regarding the injury done to the name of Asano. They seemed to be unconcerned about such matters as justice or revenge and never once even mentioned Kira's name.

Yoshida nodded. "I share your concern, my son. But look at it from their standpoint. They feel themselves so close to the brink of a new disaster—such as losing their own lives or property—that they have no desire to look back on the tragedy that brought all this about. But, even though they are in the family, we here in Ako are most immediately affected. We are the ones who are about to lose our home, not they."

Oishi agreed that he was probably right and resolved for their own sake not to involve either Daigaku or his uncle in any plan for revenge which might be formulated. In this way he could justify any call for violent action with the knowledge that they would remain blameless and Yoshida agreed that this was wise policy.

The next order of business was to give his men their final orders. When they were all assembled in front of the castle again, Oishi read Daigaku's letter to them and was depressed to see so many crestfallen faces among his warriors. It was irrevocable now that they would have to surrender, barring a last minute miracle, and they were too practical minded to believe in miracles. Oishi advised them that even if the Shogun's representatives who came to Ako received the petition favorably, they would probably not have the authority to act on it and would have to refer the matter to Edo for a final decision. So there was nothing for them to do but prepare to evacuate. The time had come to tell their families to start packing, keeping in mind that they would only be allowed to take what they could personally carry. He stressed that they must obey the Shogun's order of confiscation to the letter and do nothing that would compromise Daigaku's eventual chances of inheritance.

Now came the business of dividing the clan's monetary assets. First there were donations to the local temple to ensure that the graves of the ancestors would be well tended. Next, a sum representing Lady Asano's widow's dowry was set aside. After that the clan's paper money was redeemed at a fair rate for both retainers and townspeople alike. So far there were no complaints about the way the finances were being handled, but now, with a meaningful glance at Hara, Oishi proposed that the bulk of what was left be put aside for "the restoration of the house of Asano." As he had expected, there were mutterings from some of the men, including Ono, who had more seniority and therefore a larger share coming than most of them, but their objections became no stronger. In this company no one was bold enough to openly dispute such an allotment. What was left was then divided among the men according to rank and length of service. The amounts they received were not large and all realized that they were facing severe economic hardship if not outright destitution.

As they stepped forward politely one by one to receive their shares, Oishi pondered what was to become of them. Now they would be samurai no more, but would bear the despised title of ronin. They would be lonely men, without station or prestige, still privileged to wear their two long swords, but without any just cause to serve. No wonder it was so easy for ronin to come to bad ends, he thought. Some became beggars or priests, harmless enough pursuits, but others became professional mercenaries, fighting for any cause which paid enough to command their loyalty. In some cases they became nothing more than common criminals, using their prowess in the military arts to prey on those less strong, and Oishi realized that even the men of Ako could slip into the same pitfalls if he proved incapable of holding them together.

When all the shares had been distributed, Oishi felt called upon to say one final word. The men finished counting their money and gave him their full attention, many of them wondering if they would ever meet together again. His words were brief and to the point.

"Wherever you go, whatever you do, remember that in my mind and in our late lord's mind you are always samurai of the house of Asano. Please behave in such a way as to bring nothing but honor to the memory of this house. I know that Lord Asano is watching you at all times just as I know that he watches me. Please make his spirit happy—not sad."

There was silence for a moment and then the men began to leave. The last meeting they would ever attend in Ako was over.

"Here they come!" shouted the guard at the gate, and the word was quickly passed along to Oishi. He quickly finished his morning bowl of rice and hurried to the watchtower overlooking the plain in front of the castle. From the large cloud of dust approaching down the road it was apparent that the Shogun's troops had indeed arrived.

Swiftly now he gave the necessary orders: all men in semi-battle dress, all guard stations fully manned, all available mounts saddled and ready to ride. He himself dressed for riding, not for battle, but he also wore a thick, lacquered breastplate carrying the great gold crest of Asano. Then he joined the other horsemen mounted behind the closed gates, taking a position where he could see out through an observation slit.

Leading the advancing foot soldiers across the plain was the Shogun's representative, a distinguished-looking man in his fifties on a well-groomed horse, which he advanced at a stately walk. Oishi knew that if the men of Ako made any show of resistance the neighboring daimyo would be obliged to put their forces at the Shogun's disposal, but at the moment there was only this one small company of foot soldiers marching against him, and he had to admire the cool deliberateness of its leader.

The man on horseback continued to move forward, noting and appreciating the neat appearance of the castle and its approaches. He was more than halfway across the plain when his second in command, a plump, nervous dignitary who was also on horseback, called his attention to the castle gates which were now slowly opening.

As Oishi's group of men appeared in the opening, the breathing of the approaching troops became faster, but they relaxed again as Oishi and his men rode slowly out in strict formation, in the manner of troops on parade. The leader of the Shogun's forces noted that their horses were too well groomed, but he reflected that his own mount would not meet with the Shogun's approval either and dismissed the matter from his mind as the two groups drew nearer.

"Welcome to the castle of Asano," said Oishi in formal tones as he halted his men and saluted. The Shogun's representative stopped and bowed his head in polite acknowledgment of this courteous reception. The tension was broken and the fat little deputy commander mopped his brow.

This mutually respectful exchange set the tone for the relationship that existed during the next few days while the formalities of the transfer of ownership went on. To Oishi's satisfaction, the senior representative, whose name was Araki, was visibly impressed by the condition of the property and by the smart salutes he and his men received from the impeccable guards.

At the first opportunity, when the Edo group had had time to rest after their long journey, Oishi presented his petition. Along with it he recited the history of the Asano clan all the way back to service under the first Shogun, Ieyasu, and concluded that they were willing to make any sacrifice if Daigaku were made successor to their late beloved Lord Asano, even to committing seppuku before his grave.

Araki could not help but be impressed by the sincerity of Oishi and his men and promised to see what he could do on their behalf. He explained that he was in no position to personally make any guarantees but he would do what he could to see that the petition received proper attention at Tsunayoshi's court. He even went so far as to write a personal recommendation and dispatch it with the petition to Edo by special messenger.

Oishi was encouraged by this and felt that he could rely on Araki to follow up on the matter when he returned to Edo. There was no reason to doubt the promises made by one old warrior to another and Oishi dared to hope that something would eventually come of their plea.

The inspection of the castle and surrounding territory took five days. At the end of that time, Araki declared that as official representative of the Shogun he was satisfied that the property was accurately inventoried and in good condition. He was ready to take possession.

That night Oishi went again to Kegaku-ji, the Asano family temple. Here he found many of his men had gathered to say farewell to the ancestral tombs and to one another. Oishi personally spoke to each one and told those in his volunteer group to spread the word as to where he could be located, but asked that no one try to reach him for a period of at least two months so that a conspiracy would not be suspected. He gave each a sincere message of hope that eventually honor would be restored to their lord's name, although inwardly he could not help but feel certain misgivings about their being able to stay together as a band. He knew that separation was bound to weaken his position as leader and that discipline and morale, no matter how high now, would deteriorate with time.

The next morning at six o'clock the gates of the castle were opened and Araki's men marched in to change places with the old guard. The men of Ako and their families came out with hand-drawn carts loaded with their personal possessions and moved slowly onto the plain before the castle. There was a final formal exchange between Oishi and Araki and then the Shogun's men took possession and the gate was again closed.

Oishi and his men were silent as they looked back for the last time at what had been their invincible stronghold while the women stifled their sobs as was expected of wives and daughters of samurai. Then a baby started to cry, and to escape having to bear the unbearable the families began to move off in one direction or another, depending on where they thought their chances of making a livelihood would be best.

Oishi and his family headed for the main highway that led to Osaka and Kyoto, as did most of the others including Hara, Kataoka, and Mimura. He led his horse beside a cart piled high with luggage and his son Chikara walked beside him. Behind came his wife with three little ones, all dressed in warm traveling clothes that were very much alike. No outsider could have known that one of the three children was Lord Asano's little daughter, whom Oishi had sworn to protect with his life if necessary. He had been unwilling to give her into anyone else's care even during the period when he was dealing with Araki, preferring to take the risk and responsibility himself. He had no way of knowing what the Shogun's orders were regarding the child and preferred to let Araki think she was with her mother, which was where he intended to deliver her when the time was right.

As the castle disappeared in the dust behind them, Oishi glanced back at the little girl and saw that she was dry eyed, even as she had been when told of her father's death and her mother's exile. He was impressed by her self-control, worthy of a true daughter of a samurai, and hoped that in the uncertain future they were facing she would continue to bend like the willow before the winds of fortune.

Chapter Six

KYOTO WAS VISITED BY GREAT FLOODS that spring, which made Oishi's first move more difficult. The Kamo River, flowing through the central part of the city, overran its banks in nearly a hundred places and brought widespread death and destruction. Most of the principal foot bridges were down, and crisscrossing the area with a small child in tow was not an easy task. The one advantage was that such conditions made it harder for spies from Edo to stay on his trail, if any were in fact present.

He had brought Lord Asano's little daughter here to find a suitable home where she could be brought up as one of the family. Later, if she could not rejoin her mother, the adoption could be made permanent. The important thing was that no one must know she was an Asano, lest she fall into the Shogun's hands and be held as a hostage for Oishi and his band's good behavior.

Kyoto was still Japan's religious capital and nearly a tenth of its half-million inhabitants were priests of one sort or another. Although the influence of Buddhism was past its peak, there were still temples everywhere, not to mention large numbers of "holy men" who had established their own priesthoods and roamed the streets dressed according to their fancies.

As a city of business, Kyoto could not compare with nearby Osaka in size or capacity, but as a place of pleasure it had no rival anywhere. There were three enormous geisha districts, including the fabulous Gion quarters, and the businessmen from Osaka and other surrounding towns kept them humming with activity.

For Oishi, however, the main attraction in Kyoto was not in either its spiritual or its recreational aspects. He had come to Kyoto because it was the residence of the Emperor Higashiyama and his court, reasoning that it would be in the home of one of the Imperial courtiers that his young charge would be safest. It was well known that the Shogun wished to keep the divine person of the Emperor untroubled by the mundane affairs of government and he had therefore separated the two capitals. It was also part of the unspoken bargain that the Shogun kept his hands off the small isolated realm of the Emperor and would do nothing that could conceivably offend his court. If Lord Asano's daughter came under the protection of a member of this court, Oishi felt he could rest assured that she would be entirely safe from even the Shogun himself.

The Asano affair was well known throughout Japan by now and Oishi himself was much talked about. Fortunately, few knew him by sight and by dressing as a commoner he could move about without attracting undue attention. He stayed strictly away from his own family to avoid possible exposure to spies, but as time went by and he was still unsuccessful in finding a home for the girl, he grew more and more tempted to give up the search for a foster home and go home.

The candidates on his list of foster parents were eliminated one by one as they found some excuse or other to decline Oishi's request. Some of the reasons they gave were undoubtedly legitimate, such as simple lack of material resources, but others he suspected were motivated by the fear of becoming involved in any way with a family whose name had come under a shadow. With all his prospects Oishi took the precaution of veiling the little girl's face so that the family who eventually took her would not be embarrassed in future meetings with fellow courtiers who might remember her.

He had almost despaired of ever finding a place for her when he was directed by relatives to the home of a certain noble of samurai rank who had once been a good friend of the late Lord Asano. The man's qualifications were excellent: he held fairly high rank in the court; he had financial means to support the girl adequately, and he had several children of his own. He promised to talk the matter over with his wife and meet with Oishi and the girl on the following day.

At the appointed time they arrived at the house near the Emperor's Palace, and he left the girl in the entrance hall while he went in to discuss her future. He was disconcerted when the couple asked to see the child but he hesitated only a moment, then called her in and asked her to take off the scarf around her head. Dressed in her prettiest kimono, she was so unexpectedly charming in appearance that the family took to her at once and insisted that Oishi search no further. They would absorb her into their family group as a "cousin from the country" and no one would ever be the wiser.

Oishi was satisfied that he could not have found a better home in which to leave her, but the moment of farewell was no less poignant. The couple who were adopting her withdrew so the good-byes could be said privately but, left alone, Oishi and the girl were suddenly silent in the realization that this would be their last meeting. She turned away from him, but he could see the tears she was trying to hide.

"Bees sting a crying face," he said in as light a tone as he could manage, and the little girl bravely tried to smile.

"Uncle...uncle, please give my best regards to my mother."

Then she broke down completely and threw herself into his arms. He comforted her by assuring her he would deliver her message and then gently reminded her that as the daughter of a samurai she should have better control of her emotions. As for himself, he said, he was the same as a blood relative and did not mind her tears, but the others, the members of her new family, should not be expected to bear her troubles as well as their own. This was part of her obligation for their kindness.

Deliberately she stopped her tears and released him. She stepped back and wiped her eyes, then forced a little smile. "I will do as you say, uncle," and she delicately bowed her head. "I will do it for you."

"For your family, child," he said abruptly. "Let all your actions be guided by the honor of the name of Asano."

Then he bowed quickly, turned, and went out the door. He knew he should feel some satisfaction in having done so well, but instead found only a larger sense of desolation within himself as he returned to his wife and children.

Local relatives had obtained a house for Oishi and his family at Yamashina, a village a few miles east of Kyoto. This location had seemed ideal because of its proximity to Kyoto and Osaka, where most of the band was located, and because it was closer to Edo than either of them. The house itself was old but comfortable looking, Oishi saw as he approached it for the first time, and he was sure it could soon be put in good repair. Surrounding the property was a wall of rough stone, topped with a low solid wooden fence. On each side of the heavy wooden gate a plaster wall extended for a short distance, pierced by a long narrow window with wooden bars. There were no guards for the gates and the wall would provide no effective deterrent against a determined attack, but the arrangement did furnish some degree of privacy.

After he greeted his family and young Mimura, who would act as his household steward, Oishi toured the house and was pleased by the many rooms of various sizes, connected by narrow crooked halls. There was something of the feeling of the castle they had left in Ako and it immediately felt like home. He noted that the heavy thatched roof sagged somewhat at the gable joinings and that there were patches in the plaster here and there, but some additional strengthening of the walls should make things right and on the whole he felt grateful to his relatives for finding such a place. He assumed they had come by it through honest means out of the money he had given them, although he could never be sure about such schemers as his Kyoto cousins, the sharp-nosed Shindo and the innocent-eyed Koyama.

He was surprised to find that he had received messages from several prominent daimyo who wanted to employ him as chief retainer, but his dedication to the house of Asano had never been stronger and he answered them all with polite refusals on the grounds that his health was impaired and he would not be able to take on full-time duties of any sort for the time being. The truth was that he did have a recurrent pain in his stomach, brought on by the strain he had been under since the death of Lord Asano, but to his family he made light of it as a minor sickness of the soul that would disappear when the petition was granted.

Their first visitor in the new house was Kataoka. He had been in Osaka with Hara and was now pleased to report that his fierce old friend had found employment as an archery instructor to the townspeople and thus would be able to keep himself in excellent practice for combat.

Kataoka was dismayed to see, however, that Oishi was not pleased at this news. The thought of his prize warrior teaching commoners one of the arts formerly reserved for the samurai class did not set at all well with him, although he knew he was being foolish. He tried to convince himself that it was all for the best, but he was plainly shocked at first hearing about Hara the warrior as Hara the school teacher.

Kataoka quickly understood what his feelings were and avoided mentioning Hara's new employment from that time on. He assisted Oishi in lining up a crew of workmen to start the house repairs and for several days they were busy planning and supervising these activities. They were careful in hiring the men to question each one about his experience and place of origin, hoping to screen out any possible spies from Edo, but there was always the possibility that one could have slipped through. For this reason Kataoka kept a close watch on their comings and goings and reported to Oishi daily.

One evening after the workmen had left, Kataoka appeared before his leader with a worried look on his wizened little face. For the past two days he had noticed a flute-playing *komuso*, or itinerant priest, standing across the road from the house and just now, looking out the long narrow peephole in the wall, he had seen one of the workmen exchange words with him. The suspicious aspect of the encounter was that the priest had then led him away out of sight instead of merely accepting a donation. Oishi was thoughtful as Kataoka led him outside to the wall and showed him that the "priest" had returned. Like all those of the *komuso* variety he wore a woven reed basket over his entire head to preserve his anonymity. It was the perfect disguise for a spy, if that was indeed his business.

Oishi had to admit that the man was behaving suspiciously, but he did not know what action they could take except to note which workmen appeared to have any connection with him and to get rid of them on some pretext or other. Mindful of the fact that a word once uttered is beyond the reach of galloping horses, from this time on Oishi and Kataoka barely spoke to each other at all for fear of giving something away. Even if there were no spies, there was no point in tempting robbers. For one thing, the chest containing the funds for the "restoration of the house of Asano" was in the house and they dared not jeopardize it under any circumstances.

On August 14, spies or no spies, Oishi decided to visit the Reikoin Temple in the northern part of Kyoto. It had been five months to the day since Lord Asano's death and as other members of the Asano clan were buried here it seemed the most fitting place to observe the occasion. Besides, Oishi had arranged before leaving Ako that he would meet here with any followers who might be in the Kyoto area at this time.

He arrived early at the temple, which was in a secluded wood, and while Kataoka stayed at the entrance to guide the others to him, he went to stand among the graves of the Asanos to commune again with his lord's spirit. He respectfully reported on all that had happened to date, including the placement of the girl and the filing of the petition. He imagined that Lord Asano's spirit would be more composed now that his daughter was safe, but the basic problems remained and Oishi strengthened his resolve to eventually bring peace to his master's soul.

When the others arrived, he greeted them warmly. He was pleased to see most of the sixty-two who had given their pledge of loyalty, but the kept his remarks confined to the observance of the death day and made no reference to future plans. He did, however, ask them to meet him there each month so that they would not lose contact with one another. He exchanged individual farewells with every man present, trying to solidify the sense of purpose they all must feel if they were to succeed. The men then left by twos and threes until only Oishi and Kataoka remained. It was late at night when they went out the temple gate, but they were startled to see that a basket-headed priest was watching them from across the road.

"It may be only a coincidence," Oishi whispered. After all, there were dozens of such men in Kyoto. But then, observing Kataoka's eyes narrow menacingly, he took him by the hand and walked him away. This was not the time for a showdown.

"I'll go ahead," Oishi muttered in his companion's ear. "You wait to see if I'm followed and I'll meet you at the house."

Kataoka nodded and they split up. Now they would learn the truth about the man in the basket.

Purposely choosing a zigzag route, Oishi happened to take a turn that led through one of the principal pleasure quarters. This was a shocking experience. These places were nighttime worlds that woke sleepily in the afternoons and only really came to life when the sun went down and the huge red lanterns were lit in the narrow streets. Most apparent were the ordinary houses of prostitution, identifiable by the lone "watch-girl" who waited by the doorway to greet customers. A girl with this assignment was usually being punished by the owner of the house for some misdeed and was obliged to lie with anyone who asked for the cheapest price they offered to pay. This same system was employed all over the country and Oishi was familiar with the sight from his trips through the castle town at Ako.

Deeper into the quarters, however, were things he had never dreamed existed. He had discovered, by accident, the beautifully constructed and landscaped pleasure palaces for which Kyoto was famous—the geisha houses of Gion. Here, on the banks of the Kamo River, were the brightest, gayest spots in all the land and Oishi was uneasy as he passed their secretive walls and brightly lit entrances, so outside his own experience.

But his most vivid and disgusting impression of Gion was inspired by the low behavior of some samurai. They were loud, drunken, and brawling in the streets, and Oishi had to restrain himself from drawing his sword and teaching them a lesson in deportment. He knew, however, that if he was being spied on such an action would be a sure indication to his enemies that he was far from being resigned to a retired status. Bitterly he set his jaw and walked on, but in his heart he was cursing both the softness that had come on men of his class and the temptations of the city that they seemingly could not resist.

When he arrived back at the house, he had only a short wait until Kataoka appeared. Oishi had indeed been followed and the "priest" had again taken up his position across from the house. Oishi felt a sinking feeling in his stomach as they went out to watch him through the slit in the wall and speculate about his purposes. Whatever they were, he had seen that there was a gathering at the Reikoin Temple and he was bound to report this to his superiors.

While they were watching him, another so-called *komuso*, identically dressed, took the first man's place. It was obviously time for the changing of the guard and Kataoka pleaded with Oishi to let him follow the first man so that they could learn the identities of their enemies.

"If we know their faces, Oishi-dono, we will recognize them without their disguises. Otherwise, we will remain in the dark."

"Very well, then, go. But promise you'll take no action on your own. Any overt act against a spy will be reported to Edo and the countermeasures which could be taken against us would ruin our chances of ever surprising Kira."

Kataoka promised and they withdrew into the house where the monkey-faced man put on a dark cloak. Then he left by a rear door and circled the house to come out on the road at a point where he was shielded from view of the man on guard. The first spy had the advantage of a head start, but there was only one road from Yamashina to Kyoto, and Kataoka had no trouble picking up his trail in the bright moonlight.

As it turned out, he had only a short distance to go. The man was staying at an inn on the outskirts of Kyoto, and Kataoka drew his breath in sharply as he watched him take off his basket head-covering and drop it with his long wooden flute in the bushes outside the entrance. No one inside would be able to identify him as a "priest" in case there should be any questioning.

The man, who was tall and thin and had the aloof air of a samurai, now quickly entered the inn and Kataoka drew as close as he dared to watch and listen. Fortunately it was a warm night and the *shoji* were open all around the building. He saw his man disappear up some stairs and dashed into a side garden to watch him enter a room on the second floor. Kataoka, who was monkey-like in more ways than one, climbed to the roof of an adjoining shed, from which he was able to jump quietly into the corner of a small balcony out-side the room. There were two others present and he held his breath as he watched the men's shadows move on the balcony beside him.

The thin one he had followed wasted no time in telling the others about Oishi's activities. He had a deep bass voice that Kataoka tried to identify but could not. As he listened, he was impressed with the man's thoroughness; he even knew the names of all the men who had gathered at the temple. He also reported that he may have been spotted as a spy because of the roundabout route taken by Oishi after he left the temple, but he did not think this would do any harm. If the ex-followers of Asano knew they were being watched, there was that much more reason to think they would not behave rashly.

Now the spy dropped his priest's robe and took off his *haori* jacket. As he looked for a place to hang it he told the others that he would send a note to Edo by messenger that night. The meeting at the Reikoin Temple was the first tangible thing he had to report in all the weeks he had been watching Oishi, and he was anxious that his superiors get the message at once. Then he walked to the balcony and flung the coat across the railing almost in Kataoka's face. The monkey-faced man froze as the thin man's feet nearly brushed his own, but he was invisible in the shadows and the spy stepped back into the room without noticing him.

The others now began to comment on the report and by their voices Kataoka was able to identify one as a regular worker in Oishi's household. The other man was unknown to him, but it was apparent that both were in the service of the tall, thin one. Deciding that he had heard enough, Kataoka stood to jump from the balcony when he happened to notice the printed design on the *haori* hanging on the rail. He drew a quick breath of surprise, then recovered himself and vaulted lightly to the ground.

"It was the crest of Uesugi," he announced in a rush of words as Oishi let him in the rear entrance. "Uesugi of Yonezawa— you know the clan, they're famous for their expert archers!"

Oishi frowned. "Uesugi...yes. And our enemy Kira's grand-son was adopted into the house of Uesugi not so long ago... Horibe mentioned it in one of his reports. The chief councilor of that house, Chisaka, is very shrewd, I hear...that wasn't the name of the man you saw tonight, was it?"

"No, the others addressed him as Fujii."

"He must be a professional spy. Chisaka would employ nothing but the best."

"But why should Chisaka be so concerned with Kira's affairs just because his son is in the family now? Do we have to figure on taking on the bowmen of Uesugi, too?"

Oishi was thoughtful. "It could be. It's my guess, however, that Chisaka is trying to avoid any kind of conflict. He prob-ably considers that if Kira were attacked and killed it would reflect on his own master, Lord Uesugi, and he is therefore tak-ing every precaution to see that such a thing doesn't happen."

Kataoka nodded. This made perfect sense; the expense of the spies was worth it if it kept the mind of Chisaka's master at rest. "But what about our meetings? Will we have to avoid contact with our own men from now on?"

"We can't afford that," Oishi said firmly. "We can only hope that our gatherings become accepted as routine rituals commemorating our late master. To cut ourselves off from the men of Ako now would destroy any chance we might have for unified action later."

Kataoka accepted this but still had an uncomfortable look. Oishi noticed it and asked him what was still troubling him.

"It was the third man in the room," he said. "I'm afraid it's someone we thought we could trust."

Oishi had sickening thoughts of one of his own men going over to the enemy, but Kataoka quickly realized the impression he had given and hastened to correct it. "No, no, I didn't mean one of us. But it is someone from your household—the cook who was recommended to you by your cousin Shindo!"

"A bird flies up near one's feet," came to Oishi's lips, and he frowned to think that even his own household was not safe.

"I know you think highly of his work; it'll be too bad to have to terminate his services."

Kataoka concluded by caressing his sword hilt in an obvious gesture, but Oishi raised his hand. "No, no, you're as bad as Hara. You want to rush into action that can only get us into more trouble. What surer sign could our enemies have that we are plotting against them than if we kill their spies? No, we will keep this man on and use him for our own purposes. If the time comes that we wish false information to be circulated, we'll know exactly where to leak it to."

"Excellent," said Kataoka admiringly. "But we must warn everyone to be on his guard. Your wife and children must know what kind of thing we are concealing in the kitchen."

Oishi thought for a moment. "No, I think not. I trust them not to say anything they shouldn't, even now. If they start behaving strangely in front of the cook, he'll suspect that we suspect him and he will be of little use to us. He must believe that we know nothing. Don't you agree that that's best?"

Kataoka reluctantly nodded but still looked downcast.

"What's the matter now?" Oishi asked.

"I wish *I* didn't know about him."

"And why is that?"

"Because now my appetite will be spoiled thinking about who cooked the meal."

Oishi laughed. "Then maybe you won't eat so much and will stop getting so fat."

Kataoka made a wry face but inwardly he was smiling. He had made Oishi laugh for the first time since they had left Ako and he felt this was accomplishing a great deal under the circumstances.

The next day, however, there were two messages from Edo that stopped all laughter. The first was from Araki, who was now back in Edo. He had personally called on the Shogun's councilors to ask them to give Oishi's petition special consideration, but he frankly said there was little cause for hope. The second message was from Horibe, the acting leader of the Edo group, and it was a demand for prompt action against Kira. Oishi felt the sharp pain in his side flare up as he read it. He was sure his men in Edo were under constant surveillance by Chisaka's spies, and knew an attack at this point would be doomed to failure, but he felt helpless in explaining this to Horibe at such a distance. He was too closely followed to go to Edo himself, but somehow Horibe, an impetuous young man, must be made to understand that they had to wait for results on the petition. He finally decided that the best thing to do was send Hara, who could speak to his former comrade in arms better than anyone else. Accordingly, he asked Kataoka to do something far beyond the call of duty and take over the archery classes in Osaka. Kataoka agreed with a rueful smile, and Hara came to Yamashina for extensive briefing in Oishi's arguments before he left for Edo. He was also warned to be on guard against any tall, thin strangers with deep voices.

The next few weeks were anxious ones. In spite of Hara's strong feelings on the subject of what should be done with Kira, Oishi trusted his fierce old lieutenant to faithfully represent the opinion of his leader while dealing with Horibe. In this trust Oishi was not mistaken, but unfortunately Hara was not able to convince the young samurai in Edo that waiting was the best policy. Their tempers were riled daily by their observations of Kira and they were hot to act without delay. Accordingly, Hara wrote that in spite of all the good reasons why Oishi should not come to Edo, the situation was so serious he had better make the trip anyway.

This message upset Oishi tremendously. He was gravely concerned lest the Edo group go ahead and take action on its own and he finally decided, after first cursing Hara for a fool, that his reasoning was sound and that the sooner he went the better. There were other things he could take care of in Edo at the same time, and so in any event the trip would not be wasted.

Chapter Seven

FOR HIS AIDES ON THE TRIP, Oishi decided to take his Kyoto relatives, Shindo and Koyama. Neither of them were to his taste as traveling companions, but because they were not ex-retainers of Lord Asano a visit to Edo with them was less likely to be construed as warlike. Also, although they had sworn allegiance to his cause, he felt they lacked real dedication and that exposure to the fanatical Edo group might heighten their sense of purpose.

They set out on the Tokaido—the road to the eastern sea—in late October, at a time when the hills were afire with the flaming colors of autumn and the days had become cool enough so that the weather on the long journey would be comfortable. It was still an ordeal for Oishi to sit all day on top of a pile of bedding laid over a pack saddle with his legs crossed or else hanging down by the horse's neck in the cavity between the trunks on each side. The pace was slow and Oishi and his companions rocked endlessly back and forth under their large straw umbrella hats. They made no attempt to disguise themselves, as this would only give an impression of secrecy they were anxious to avoid.

There were fifty-three posts, or barriers, between Kyoto and Edo with the leagues marked by small tree-topped hills. For shade there were straight rows of firs planted on each side of the winding two-lane road. There were also huts of green-leaved branches every two or three leagues where the travelers could relieve themselves in special receptacles in order that the excreta could be used by the local farmers as fertilizer. Oishi was appalled to find that many of them had not been emptied in some time, and horse droppings along the way had also been allowed to stand. It was plain that many farmers along the way had given up the struggle against an army of pests they were forbidden to battle effectively.

The towns they passed through were much alike. There were no walls or moats surrounding them, but generally there were large wooden gates at either end of town with a section of wall extending for a short distance on each side. Some of the villages were merely one long street with shops on both sides. The structures were low with thatched or shingled roofs and open to the street, with rows of straw ropes hanging down to keep the passers-by from looking in. By the side of the entrance there was usually a picture of the household god, generally a dragon or a devil.

The streets in the towns were always crowded and noisy, and Oishi and his party were badgered by more beggars than he had ever seen before. The sellers of various merchandise shouted to them as they passed and there were innumerable funeral processions with loud singing and wailing by the priests and the relatives of the dead. The keepers and inmates of the brothels also cried out loudly for the travelers to stop and enjoy themselves, but Oishi continually kept his face to the front and his companions were obliged to do likewise, at least during the day.

At nightfall Oishi sought a quiet inn on the outskirts of town where he hoped to get a good night's rest, but in this he was disappointed. Here, too, female companionship was available for those who wanted it. The market was glutted with farmers' daughters and they had even moved into what were once respectable hotels and inns. For Oishi the visit to Edo where his master was buried had the character of a religious pilgrimage, but for his companions it was merely a holiday and they kept him awake half the night with their drunken parties.

He was awakened one morning by a woman's shriek that had him scrambling for his sword before the cry turned to giggling, and he realized the party had begun again. He shook his head in disgust and decided the time had come to teach his companions a lesson they would not forget.

They had not been long out of Yamashina when it became apparent to Oishi that they were being followed. A certain tall, thin samurai and a companion came in sight behind them on the road and stopped whenever they did. It was undoubtedly Fujii, as Kataoka had described him.

At first Oishi decided not to mention the matter to Shindo and Koyama, who appeared blissfully unaware of what was happening, but their perpetual party-making caused him to change his mind.

That morning on the road he deliberately shortened the distance between his group and the spy Fujii who was following them. Then he picked an inn for the noonday meal in a place where it would have been awkward for Fujii to turn back or go ahead to eat elsewhere. The two parties thereby found themselves seated side by side on the same open porch facing away from the highway toward the red-and-yellow hills. Shindo and Koyama were enjoying both the scenery and the meal and already making plans for another fun-filled evening when Oishi rose and excused himself to go and wash up. As he walked past Fujii, however, he deliberately tripped himself and fell against the startled spy.

Fujii leaped to his feet with a deep-voiced curse and whipped out his sword in the same motion. He stood glowering at the apologetic Oishi until a sudden suspicion came to his mind that the fall had been no accident. Then he smiled an apology of his own and sat down. He was chagrined that his usefulness as a spy had been impaired, but he knew there were ways to make use of this new situation, too.

As for Shindo and Koyama, the sight of the crest on the thin man's sword did not escape them. It was plainly the mark of the house of Uesugi, and they lost their appetites when they saw it. Both now recollected that they had seen this man on the road behind them since leaving Yamashina and realized the precariousness of their situation. In the eyes of Oishi's enemies they were now marked as his collaborators, with whatever consequences that might bring, and their attitudes became more sober and silent.

On another morning, when they were about halfway to their destination, Oishi had another opportunity to teach them a lesson. They came to the outskirts of one more town like the rest, but as they approached it from the west they passed the traditional location of the execution grounds, which had recently been put to use. The body of a crucified prisoner presented a gruesome sight in the sunlight, bound to a wooden cross and pierced with lances.

"I see there is work for the *eta*, even if the tanning of leather is no longer permitted," Oishi said in a grim joke about the outcasts of society who were only permitted to hold jobs as leather workers or executioners.

His companions wet their lips and were silent as Oishi guided his horse closer to the corpse.

"'Executed for counterfeiting,'" he read from the poster. "Well, that's not uncommon nowadays—when the government keeps debasing our currency, you're bound to find those willing to take a chance and defy the Shogun's edicts."

Shindo and Koyama muttered to each other under their breaths and Oishi pressed home his point about the consequences of illegal acts. "Kill a fox, kill a dog, kill a man—the penalty is the same for all such crimes, no matter what the provocation."

The sharp-faced Shindo pursed his lips tightly and Koyama's jaw hung open more slackly than usual as they rode on. They knew what Oishi was telling them; that a similar fate was awaiting for those who followed him and took illegal revenge. Oishi did not want to discourage them but he did want them to realize what might be in store for them. If they were not up to it, the sooner they found out and left his band.

The journey went on, past stately Buddhist *tera* (temples) with their carved idols and smell of sweet-scented candles, past smaller Shinto *miya* (shrines), seen through their magnificent torii. There were also stone images of Jizo along the way. Over the rivers which were not too swift, or did not radically alter their courses from season to season, there were fine cedar bridges with rails. Over others, where the bridges had been washed out, it was necessary to take flat-bottomed ferryboats, and to cross the Oigawa River between Totomi and Suruga as they neared Edo it was necessary to ford the river as there were neither bridges nor boats available.

They came in sight of Mt. Fuji, dead ahead, then watched it move slowly to their left as they approached the Kanto Plain on which Edo was located. The last climb was over the Hakone Pass where the autumn scenery was magnificent and the view of Fuji unparalleled, but the travelers' minds were too full of their own problems to appreciate their surroundings. No matter how spectacular their beauty, the deer hunter never sees the mountains.

In Edo, Kira's mouth went dry with fear when he learned that Oishi was on his way. He went at once to the castle of Uesugi to see Chisaka, whose messenger had brought him the bad news.

"Ah, Chisaka-san, you're looking well," he began with a forced smile that showed his blackened teeth.

"And so are you, Lord Kira," the oily, balding little councilor replied. "Yet there are rumors that you are thinking of retiring because of poor health. Can this be true?"

Kira moved uncomfortably. It was true he had been asked to retire because of the notoriety he had attained in the Asano affair, but he had hoped to keep it a secret a while longer. He might have known that Chisaka would find out before anyone else.

"An old ailment has returned," he said. "I have no choice... But that reminds me of something I want to ask you about. Since I'll be leaving the Shogun's castle, I'll be needing some place to stay and I wondered if..."

"I'll personally help you find a house," Chisaka interrupted, anxious to keep Kira from moving into his own master's castle.

"But I need more than a house," Kira insisted. "I need guards on duty at all times and a place for them to stay."

Then he added in a softly insinuating manner: "Not that I'm afraid for myself, you understand, but after all, our houses are related and I wouldn't want Lord Uesugi to be embarrassed by an incident."

"You'll get everything you need," Chisaka promised hastily, although inwardly he was groaning at the thought of the expense. It was worth it to him only if it accomplished the purpose of keeping Kira and his problems at a distance. The Asano affair was turning out to be a troublesome problem, but for the time being at least he could do nothing but put up with it.

"And now that matters are settled, won't you have some tea?" he asked his guest with a forced smile.

Kira hesitated, then forced a black smile of his own.

"Why not? We should become better acquainted since I'm sure we'll be seeing much more of each other in the future."

And they sat down together as Chisaka summoned a servant to bring them tea, however bitter it might taste to both of them.

Chapter Eight

TWELVE DAYS FROM THE TIME Oishi's group left Kyoto they arrived in Edo, their entourage intact, including the spy Fujii who now kept a more respectful distance between them. On their way into the city, they paused briefly at Sengaku-ji, a small temple and burial ground where Lord Asano was buried. Here Oishi went alone to pour purifying water from a slender bamboo dipper over the base of the stone marker. Then he left the grave wearily after bowing deeply and reassuring his lord that he could be depended upon as always.

He rejoined the others outside the temple and they proceeded into the city. The unfamiliar streets were crowded and noisy, and Oishi shuddered at the disquieting press of humanity on all sides. It was getting late in the day when they found a small downtown inn and settled for the night. He was in no great hurry to confront his rebellious followers, and besides, there was another important visit he had to make after resting and dressing in something more seemly than his traveling clothes. His stomach was hurting him again so he ate little and went to bed early. Even after dark, however, the streets of the city rang with the barking of the dogs, and he tossed restlessly. He had never felt at ease in Edo and it was not until he turned his thoughts to Yamashina and his family that his mind became composed and he at last fell asleep.

The next day he paid the call he had been looking forward to—he went to visit Lady Asano at the home of her parents. He was not sure he would be allowed to see her, but happily he found no guards present and was taken to her without incident.

She was dressed in a nunlike robe and her manner was subdued as she received him in the small bare room off the garden into which she had exiled herself. There were Buddhist sutras lying on the floor by the writing table and Oishi surmised that she spent her days and nights patiently copying them, hoping to find some peace of mind from the tragedy that had overtaken her.

"I hope all your family is well," she said with an unaccustomed smile, and he knew she was really asking about her own daughter.

"They are all well—even the little one who has gone to stay with friends." He had written to her earlier of course about the adoption, but knew that words on a page are a poor substitute for personal assurances.

"Have you seen her lately?"

"No, my lady, I think it best that I stay away lest others learn of my unusual interest in the daughter of an Imperial courtier. At the least I would be accused of meddling in politics."

He tried to make a joke of it but there was no smile on Lady Asano's face as she continued to ask questions all around the subject of her daughter's whereabouts. "And is this Imperial courtier quite high up in the court?"

"Quite high up," Oishi said briefly, determined for her own sake and for that of her daughter never to reveal the name of the man who had adopted her.

"Then I'm sure she'll have the advantage of a good education, as befits a child of nobility," Lady Asano said with a hopeful note in her voice.

"I'm sure she will," he agreed and then turned the discussion to the petition. Lady Asano asked polite questions but her enthusiasm seemed feigned, and Oishi was discouraged to see that she had little faith that what had been done under the law would be undone. Without giving away any hint of his plans he simply told her that he was still his lord's follower and would always remain so. For a moment her thoughts turned outward from herself and she saw him in the role he had chosen—that of the last defender of the name of Asano who would carry that banner as long as there was the breath of life in him. She asked him to wait a moment and went into another room. When she came back she had a letter. It was the one Lord Asano had written the night before he died and she asked Oishi to take it with him and read it. When he left, her cheeks were stained with tears but she was smiling more peacefully, and he told himself that his visit had not been in vain. He also told himself that he must never come here again in order to avoid implicating her in his future actions.

On the way out he asked to be shown around the grounds by a servant and noted the locations of the various gates. He had it in the back of his mind that someday he would bring mother and daughter together again, although he had not mentioned any such plan to Lady Asano for fear of arousing false hopes.

The same day Oishi went to see Araki at his home to thank him for his efforts and to learn how the petition was faring. Araki received him cordially, pleased to see by Oishi's manner that he was not in Edo on a mission of protest or violence. As always, he was conducting himself with the dignity expected of a chief retainer, and Araki was more impressed with him than ever. Unfortunately, the graying old soldier had nothing promising to report; the councilors were taking their time about disposing of the case and he could only apologize for the inconvenience it was causing. They had tea together, discussed the local weather, and parted on a note of mutual understanding. This, Oishi reflected, was better than nothing, but hardly gave him ammunition for his coming encounter with his young rebels.

Courtesy demanded that he make one more call while he was in Edo. The official spokesmen for the house of Asano were Daigaku Asano and his uncle Lord Toda, and it was to the mansion of the latter that he now made his way.

It was a large estate, although in somewhat run-down condition, and Oishi made an expression of distaste as he stepped over the body of a mangy dog at the threshold. It might have been sleeping or dead, but in either case he took it as a bad omen.

His visit was unexpected and he found that Lord Toda was out. Daigaku, however, still under official house arrest, was glad to receive him as a visitor. He was a thin, nervous young man who danced around uttering little cries of welcome while his close-set eyes darted over Oishi's face to find a clue to his true intentions. Finally he stopped, laid a finger along-side one nostril, and sniffed vigorously.

"I'm so glad to see you," he repeated for the tenth time. "It's been so long."

Oishi nodded formally. "I trust Your Lordship has been well."

"I'm afraid I haven't been...these pains in my chest...I really don't know what to do for them."

"We've all been under a strain," Oishi told him. "You'll feel better when things are back to normal again."

"If they ever are," Daigaku said bitterly. "But that's something that may never happen."

"You've had no encouragement about your appointment as your brother's successor?"

"No—but Lord Toda tells me I still have a chance." Then he added hastily, "That's why we must wait and see. There's no point in jeopardizing my chances."

"No, of course not..."

They were interrupted by a sound in the hallway and in a moment Lord Toda entered in some haste. Daigaku smiled in relief. He was glad to have his uncle present during Oishi's visit.

Lord Toda, a short bristling man with a no-nonsense manner, was the complete opposite of his ineffectual young nephew. He came directly to the point with Oishi after they had exchanged bows and formal greetings.

"I hear there is agitation among some of your men for action against Kira."

Oishi looked at him closely, then nodded. "There are many who feel that to take the life of the miserable scoundrel who caused our master's death is the only honorable path to follow."

Lord Toda snorted. "Insanity...sheer insanity. Don't they know Kira lives within the Shogun's walls? Do they have any idea how thick those walls are and how well guarded?"

"They are aware of those facts, Lord Toda, but perhaps at a later date..."

"Nonsense," Toda interrupted him. "The Shogun's orders to the men of Ako were to surrender and disband and that must be the end of it...I hear you did a fine job of transferring the castle and I thank you for it. That's the kind of action that will save our family name. Not causing more bloodshed like that hot-headed young..."

He was about to say Lord Asano's name, but stopped when he saw the look in Oishi's eyes.

"Well, no matter. What's done is done. But at least we can do everything in our power to keep things from getting worse."

"And what of Lord Daigaku's chances of succession?" Oishi asked politely, determined to hear all viewpoints on this vital question.

Lord Toda paced up and down the room. "I believe the chances are good—providing we do nothing to upset the Shogun further. When time has passed and tempers have had a chance to cool, I think everyone will look at this matter in a different light. With our long history of faithful service, I can't believe we could lose everything overnight. But patience must be our watchword." He paused to look at Oishi closely. "Patience and forbearance at all times—that's how we'll win our goal."

Oishi bowed politely and Lord Toda seemed satisfied that he had understood. Tea was served and a short while later Oishi left. He was thinking that he was glad he had confronted the old man and the young heir if only to see how weak they were. It was plain that the responsibility for revenge was his alone.

That night a tall, thin man wearing the two swords of a samurai called at the castle of Uesugi and was admitted to an audience with the chief councilor, Chisaka.

"At your service," the tall man said with a deep voice, and bowed low to his diminutive superior.

"Well, and where is he now?" Chisaka demanded to know. "I trust you have him under constant surveillance?"

"I know exactly where he is. At a meeting in a restaurant in the suburbs."

"A meeting?"

"A meeting with the Ako men who stayed behind in Edo when their master was killed."

"Executed, you mean. And why aren't you at the meeting, learning about their plans?"

"I wasn't invited," said Fujii drily. "Besides they know my face now and aren't likely to take me into their confidence."

Chisaka was about to pose another ill-tempered question but Fujii anticipated him.

"Never fear—the meeting is being covered by one of my men disguised as a servant, although I doubt if he'll learn much of value."

Chisaka looked at him coldly. "You just take care of the spying, Fujii. I'll decide what's of value."

Fujii silently bowed, but Chisaka thought he detected a sardonic grin on the thin man's face.

"What makes you so sure they're not plotting to attack Kira right now?" the little man cried out in irritation.

Fujii paused, then shrugged.

"They have an intelligent leader—one who won't let them act out of rashness. And what can they do about removing Kira's head while he's safe in the castle?"

Chisaka smiled condescendingly. "You'd better leave the conjecturing to me, my friend. I have other sources of information besides you and am in a better position to fit the pieces together."

Fujii smiled uncertainly. Perhaps he had gone too far with his sarcasm.

"I'm sorry if I offended you. In the future I'll stick to my part of the job," he said, with only the faintest trace of the distaste he felt.

"Right," Chisaka agreed. "And if you do well, there'll be a permanent place for you here, as I promised. We were fortunate to have discovered each other when we did. A ronin with knowledge of the Kyoto area was what I needed just when you needed a roof over your head."

Fujii was silent. He did not like to be reminded of his past.

"Now, will you do as I say and get back on the job?"

As Fujii scrambled to bow low, Chisaka threw him the tidbit of information he had been saving.

"You see, my uninformed friend, things are a little more precarious now since Kira is no longer staying in the castle!"

"It's true," Horibe said, his topknot trembling, "Kira is no longer in the castle!"

He stood before a group of fifteen loyal Ako men, including Oishi and Hara and seven others from Kyoto and Osaka. The room he had rented for the occasion was over a noisy restaurant which allowed them to speak without fear of being overheard, and now there was a general murmur of excitement at his words.

"Then what are we waiting for?" cried one of the Edo group. "Let's attack now!"

Oishi's heart leaped, too, but he deliberately forced himself to think rationally. He rose before the group and they became quiet again in the face of his authority.

"You fools," he said coldly. "What kind of fighting force do you call yourselves, ready to go off half-cocked at any new rumor! If Horibe can confirm this news it will certainly influence our plans, but don't forget that our main body of troops is faraway at the moment and we'll need every man of them if we are to succeed." He paused to take a breath, then nodded to Horibe to continue.

"Kira," the young man said with a grimace that would have chilled the blood of the man he named, "is about to be relieved of his official duties. He was moved this morning into the suburbs on the far side of the Sumida River. I followed him there myself."

"You have done your work well," Oishi acknowledged.

Horibe smiled, but it was not a pleasant smile. "I can tell you many things about Kira," he said, and then set forth in detail what he had learned about Kira's treatment of Lord Asano, about his record of corruption in the office and even about the system of defenses at his new home. Although he had a company of archers at his disposal and was reputedly an excellent swordsman, Kira was plainly afraid of them.

As Horibe concluded his report with a threat to justify such fears, the grizzled Hara felt obliged to express his feelings.

"There are those in Osaka who say even now that we have no real intention of doing anything about taking revenge. Hasn't the time come to show them they are wrong?" He refrained from looking at their leader and was unaware of how deeply his words hurt him, but Oishi, as always, put his personal feelings aside. He patiently explained to them all once more that the welfare of their lord's house came first and that meant waiting for a decision on the petition. He knew it was difficult for them to maintain themselves in a state of readiness for an attack which might never be made, but as their leader he had to ask it.

"But don't you see," cried Horibe, "this is only a tactic on the part of the councilors. They have no intention of ever giving the land to Daigaku. They're deliberately stalling to lead us into the confused state in which we find ourselves. They know that waiting will lower our morale and eventually destroy us. We are only playing into their hands by doing nothing!"

Oishi sighed and turned to confront him. "But we're under constant surveillance. At Yamashina we're spied on around the clock and we were followed all the way to Edo. You here in Edo must be under even stricter watch. Don't you realize that at the first sign of an attack, the alarm would be flashed to Kira's powerful relatives to come and save him? Would you go to the scene of a fire in a straw raincoat? Where would our men's morale be after a futile attempt on Kira's life left the streets red with their blood?"

There was a light knock at the door and all fell silent as the man nearest the entrance admitted a servant with more tea. The man entered and moved so slowly that Hara growled at him until he took the hint and speeded up his action. Then they waited until he was let out the door.

"We know there are spies," muttered Horibe with a glance after the servant, "but we can avoid them if our plans are made carefully. I'm not asking that we attack tonight or tomorrow, but I do say that a date should be set—certainly no later than next March. In case you've forgotten, that's the anniversary of our lord's death and by then Kira must certainly be dealt with in one way or another. Can anyone persuade himself that we can wait more than a year and still maintain our reputations as brave men?"

The others agreed so vigorously that Oishi kept silent, desperately trying to think of some way to avoid committing himself. They were plainly all against him, even Hara, whom he had counted on for some support. It had probably been a mistake to send Hara here in the first place where he could be so easily inflamed by the fiery tempers of the younger men. Still, he had been successful in keeping them from acting on their own and that was something to be thankful for. Perhaps Horibe was right and there would be some decision before March. In any event he now realized that he could no longer stand against them.

"Very well," he said, disguising his reluctance and his true intentions. "We will plan on settling this matter in March. I will return to Yamashina and begin to prepare."

The others were overjoyed to hear this long awaited signal for action and shouted noisily and clapped one another on the back. Oishi was silent until Hara approached him, once more apologetic, to raise a cup of saké in a toast.

"To our success?" he said.

"To our success," Oishi agreed and downed his cup in one swift gulp. Although he had not mentioned it to anyone, Lord Asano's last letter was heavy on his mind. He had read it the night before and it had inflamed him against Kira more than ever before. He wondered if Lady Asano had given it to him for that purpose. Was she, too, for swift revenge, regardless of the consequences? He knew he would never let her down, but he also knew that he would not move until the time was right, no matter what pressures were brought to bear.

Chapter Nine

THE JOURNEY BACK TO KYOTO was uneventful. Fujii and his aide followed them, but never very closely, and much of the tension which had gripped them on their ride to Edo was gone. The three travelers were deep in their own thoughts and Shindo and Koyama, as Oishi had planned, were more impressed with the implications of their commitment. They were all glad to get home.

The year was drawing to a close and the hill colors changed from the reds of fall to the whites of winter. New Year's Day came and with it the seasonal celebrations, although Oishi did not think it fitting for his house to participate. Looking out through the gate the children could see the men in their pleated skirts and crested coats making calls at friends' homes and the women in elaborate kimono welcoming their guests. The boys in the neighborhood flew kites with knives fastened to the pulling cords to cut their opponents' strings in aerial battle and the girls in new sashes played with the traditional shuttlecocks.

It was the time for old retainers and servants to call and pay their respects and be treated for once like any other guest, but this year the house in Yamashina knew none of these pleasures.

Oishi let it be known that his family was still in mourning for the death of Lord Asano and prohibited his children from leaving the grounds. His excuse was partially true, but he also wanted them kept close for their own safety. He would not put it past Chisaka to try to take a child as hostage to keep Oishi from causing trouble for his master.

Later in January there was an urgent message from Horibe, and Hara came in a rush from Osaka when he heard about it. Kira was now officially retired and the rumor was that he was going to be invited to live at Yonezawa, in the fief of the Lord of Uesugi. In view of the strength of Uesugi's troops, this would put Kira in as safe a place as the Shogun's castle and Horibe was determined that they must act before such a move could be made.

Hara, too, urged Oishi to attack or forever regret this missed opportunity. The time to act was now and they should all be readying their weapons and preparing for the march to Edo.

Oishi, however, still convinced that they must wait for action on the petition, did not agree that this was the time. Horibe had to be stalled again somehow, but he knew that if he went to Edo himself he might be pressured into unwise decisions. As a substitute, he decided to send Yoshida, the elder statesman of the group, who agreed with his views and whose voice would carry the most weight next to his own. The point of the stratagem was that Oishi was the only one who could legitimately make a final decision and, if he were not there, perhaps Horibe could again be curbed.

At Hara's insistence, he was allowed to accompany Yoshida as his "bodyguard," although Oishi would rather he had remained at the archery school. There was always the danger that the rubbing together of two firebrands like Horibe and Hara would strike a flame that would be inextinguishable, but Oishi kept this fear to himself.

After they had gone, Kataoka prepared to leave for Osaka to take Hara's place, but delayed his departure when he sensed that Oishi needed his ear as a sounding board.

Oishi was not only concerned about what was going on in Edo, but for some reason the surveillance of the house seemed to be stricter than ever and shadowy figures followed everyone who left the house on no matter how trivial an errand. This activity both troubled and puzzled Oishi. Why at this late date should the spy forces be reinforced unless they were expecting an attack? And why should Oishi and his men plan to attack at this time? There was only one answer: Kira's move to the relatively unprotected suburbs. The obvious thing for Kira's protectors to do then was to move him without delay into a safer place, such as the castle at Yonezawa. But the fact that they only sent more spies instead of taking such an obvious move signaled something of their strategy to Oishi and he called on Kataoka to listen to his reasoning.

"Kira would be safe from any attack we might mount if he were living at Yonezawa, wouldn't you say so?" he asked.

"Yes, I suppose so," answered the somewhat mystified Kataoka.

"Therefore, if Chisaka was planning to move Kira there, there would be no reason for all this spying, would there?"

"No—I suppose not."

"Then doesn't it stand to reason," said Oishi triumphantly, "that he's not planning to move Kira at all!"

Kataoka looked at him blankly as Oishi went on to explain.

"It would be just like a schemer like Chisaka to do something like this. Of course he must protect Kira if he's obviously in danger, but to take him under his master's roof would be against his principles of caution in keeping out of harm's way. In other words, to take Kira in would be to directly involve the Lord of Uesugi in the Asano matter and that's just what Chisaka is trying to avoid."

Kataoka looked dubious for a moment, then slowly smiled and nodded his head. "You just may be right," he admitted.

"I know I am," said Oishi enthusiastically, and he went to write out his ideas for Yoshida in Edo to give him ammunition for what he knew must be a ticklish debate. The letter was never sent, however, as a message arrived from Yoshida that changed all plans.

The first part of Yoshida's letter was analytical; it described the factions represented in Edo with such acumen that Oishi was glad he had sent the old man in his place. One faction, represented primarily by Yoshida himself, supported Oishi's view that they should wait for a decision on the restoral of the house before taking any other action. Horibe's faction, of course, was for immediate action regardless of the consequences. A third group consisted of those apparently willing to wait with Oishi, but in Yoshida's eyes these men had no real stomach for revenge, whether Daigaku became heir or not. This group would stand by Oishi now, but should the petition be denied Yoshida felt they would fall away like the leaves from a tree in a frost. Oishi had to admit to himself that there probably were such men, and Yoshida was in a better position to smell them out than he was.

The second part of the letter was more upsetting, especially in view of the increased spy activity around the house. Because of the deadlock the latest series of meetings in Edo had produced, and because Oishi could not or would not come to Edo himself to resolve them, Horibe's group proposed to come to Yamashina instead. Oishi was angry about the implied snub to his chosen spokesman, Yoshida, but there was nothing to be done as the men were already on their way. As a final gesture of disrespect, Yoshida reported that Horibe had announced that he could not leave the responsibility of watching Kira to anyone else, and was sending Hara to speak for him.

Oishi was furious at this disregard of his own authority but there was nothing he could do. He could not repudiate Horibe's standing as a member of the band because of his following of young, eager fighters who might make the difference between eventual success and failure. So, although he shook his head privately, he behaved before the others as though Horibe had acted in the best interests of all.

The group arrived in February and at the first meeting at the house of Yamashina, Hara, with the bit in his teeth, wasted no time in asking why equipment was not being procured for the attack. Oishi calmly replied that he would do nothing until there was some final word about Daigaku and admitted that he had never had any serious intention of launching a March attack—he had only gone along with the others in order to stall Horibe and the other fanatics. Hara flushed to hear himself described in such terms but he pressed a fresh argument that Horibe had formulated. Suppose Daigaku was named heir and the house of Asano restored, could they then raid and kill without again bringing ruin on the very name they had waited to restore? Would there then be no revenge?

Oishi sighed and thought carefully about his answer before he spoke.

"In my mind," he finally said, "the restoration of the house and the revenge are two separate things. You are right, Hara, that if the house is restored it would be an ungrateful act for the men of Ako to go ahead and attack one of the Shogun's officials, or ex-officials, in force."

Hara's eyebrows raised at this unexpected frankness but he kept silent to hear what Oishi's solution was.

"Therefore I have resolved that if that time ever comes, I personally will take revenge on behalf of us all."

There was a pause while his words sunk in and then Hara raised his voice in a howl of frustration. "Don't you see, Oishi, that if you do that, the rest of us will be branded as cowards?"

There was a loud murmur of approval of Hara's words. "Everyone knows that a samurai cannot live under the same sky as the slayer of his lord. We must *all* be given the chance to attack, whatever the consequences are."

There were loud cries of agreement from all sides and only Yoshida and Onodera, another elder statesman, stood by Oishi. They tried to tell the others that sword rattling was not the only way to play the part of a loyal samurai and that Oishi's plan had the virtue of getting them everything they said they wanted, but such rational arguments were not heeded in the charged atmosphere of this gathering.

Oishi could see that the situation was out of control and likely to remain that way unless one side or the other gave in. It was plain to see that the others would not so he resolved to defer to their wishes as gracefully as possible in the interests of unity.

"All right," he said, raising his hand for silence, "all right. I cannot stand against so many. I agree that we will all share our fortunes together, but I still insist we must wait for the outcome of the petition. If we do not hear by March, we must wait another year. If there is no decision by then, we will assume that hope is lost forever and attack in a body. Do you understand? I promise you that at that time, or sooner, we will attack!"

The men cheered and began an excited discussion. Oishi advanced his views about Chisaka's probable attitude toward Kira, and they agreed that his analysis made sense. This information would help placate Horibe along with the news that there would be definite action forthcoming. They all renewed their pledge to stand together as a loyal band and Yoshida was sent back to Edo with instructions to stay there with Horibe until further notice. Hara returned to Osaka while Onodera, a quick, wiry old campaigner, stayed at Yamashina with Oishi as chief of staff. The men drifted away in twos and threes to make matters more difficult for the spies waiting outside, but many of them were followed and their actions reported promptly to Chisaka, and through him to Kira. When he heard about the meeting, Kira insisted that the spy force be even further augmented and Chisaka finally agreed. But he said nothing that could be construed by Kira as an invitation to move into the castle at Yonezawa.

Chapter Ten

SPRING CAME WETLY TO THE KYOTO AREA with heavy rainfall and repeated flood conditions. Oishi was confined closely to the house at Yamashina with plenty of time to think and consequently to brood. He felt hemmed in and on the defensive because of the continued presence of Chisaka's spies. He could well sympathize with Horibe and the others in Edo who kept close watch on Kira and were therefore tempted beyond the bounds of reason to strike out against him. Here in Yamashina, Oishi had no more formidable opponents to face than shadowy spies, but by the time the weather had cleared and the flood damage was repaired, he had decided on an unusual plan. Although not as dangerous as physical combat, it entailed risks of a different sort, which Oishi felt were worth taking. A sword is not always required in order to do battle.

During the first week in April he stayed late in Kyoto for several nights without explanation, but on the occasion of Kataoka's next visit in May his motives began to become apparent.

"I'm glad to see you," he greeted his old friend, with an expression more intense than usual.

"No word from Edo about the petition yet?" the monkey-faced man asked as they entered the house.

"No," Oishi growled, "and it doesn't look like there's going to be. Horibe and the others were right—the councilors are only stalling."

"You don't know that..." Kataoka began, but Oishi interrupted him.

"Don't try to salve my vanity. I admit I was wrong. I was so hopeful of saving something of what was dear to us that I blinded myself to the real truth."

"There may still be a chance. Araki said..." But again Kataoka was cut short.

"Araki doesn't make the decisions. He's been polite, possibly helpful, but we can't depend on his optimism. No, from now on we must assume that all is lost and plan accordingly."

"You mean attack now?" asked Kataoka incredulously.

Oishi hesitated, then spoke in a low voice, "When in haste it is sometimes best to take a roundabout way. There are certain preliminaries I had postponed till now but I see they can no longer wait. Get your house in order, my friend, as quickly as possible, and I shall do likewise."

They went to bed, Kataoka still puzzled about Oishi's meaning, but the next day revealed that he was indeed in earnest about settling his affairs.

In the morning Oishi rose early, as usual, to eat the morning meal with his wife and children. When it was finished and he had watched the little ones go off to play, he asked his wife to come out of the kitchen where she was helping the cook prepare the day's menu, and led her into a sitting room in another part of the house. It was late spring and he threw open the paper *shoji* to the garden, now beginning to warm in the sun. He motioned for her to sit down and she knelt obediently before him, curious and not a little apprehensive about what her husband was going to say.

"The weather has become much warmer," he said, aware of her uneasiness.

"Yes," she murmured, keeping her eyes lowered, "the buzzing of the cicadas increases with the approach of summer."

Without responding he looked at her for a moment in silent admiration. In all the years he had known her she had always behaved in exactly the correct manner for one of her station, and he knew he could depend on her to do so in the future. It was fortunate that at a time like this he could rely on her help, no matter what he asked. What he had to say now would put her training as the wife of a samurai to its severest test, yet he had faith in her ability to meet it.

"I am sorry if my coming in late has troubled you," he said, postponing the main issue but feeling that this was also something that had to be said.

"Not at all," she lied, with a quick little look up at his face. "The children and I sleep undisturbed by anything."

He knew this was a reference to the fact that he had not been to her bed for many weeks, and cleared his throat in embarrassment.

"I—what I have to ask is not easy, considering that I have no fault to find with you..."

"Anything you desire," she murmured.

"I have written out this letter," he said, producing it from his long sleeve and handing it to her. "It is a letter of divorce."

She took it in silence although her face went pale and Oishi realized that her heart must have turned to stone at his words. Without any expression she read it through, then laid it beside her on the straw-matted floor. She turned her head away and Oishi moved to the open *shoji* to look out into the garden and avoid seeing her tears.

"You must have known it would come to this," he said gently.

"I told myself that it would not," she said, controlling her voice so that not the breath of a sob would be heard. "I told myself that the petition would be granted and that we would all go home to Ako someday."

"I told myself that, too, but now the time for fairytales is over. I must do things in which I have no right to involve you and the children. That is why we must separate."

For a moment she was at a loss for words. "Involve me? Why should I not be involved in what you do?"

"Because it would not please me to have you do so," he answered and she obediently bowed her head. She had not meant to argue or oppose him.

"I want you to take the children and return to your parents' home. Whatever I do in the future will therefore not reflect on you, nor will you be held in any way responsible for my deeds. That is the way it must be if I am to feel free to act as I think I must."

"The children," she said. "Do you mean all the children?"

"Chikara is sixteen," he replied. "I think we must let him make up his own mind whether he will go or stay."

She bowed her head in final acquiescence but could not prevent a sob from escaping her.

"I must lose you both?" she suddenly cried out. For a moment there was no sound but the humming of the insects in the garden, and then she deliberately dried her eyes and composed herself.

"I am sorry," she said. "I know it is something you must do and I will pray for your success as I always have. But...when must this...divorce...happen?" she asked in a tired, faraway voice.

"Soon—as soon as possible... Please, send in Chikara so that I can put the matter to him."

Their conversation was over and she obediently bowed her head to the floor, then stood and went out, her white-stockinged feet rustling over the *tatami* in a cadence that was distinctively her own and that Oishi knew he would miss more than anything in the days ahead.

Chikara was troubled by his mother's manner when she summoned him, and went to see his father in some trepidation. He kneeled and bowed respectfully and then waited for whatever rebuke he must hear. The fact that his father's opening words were delivered in a calm, contemplative manner did not lessen his anxiety.

"Hardship in our present life is an atonement for sins committed in our previous existence, or the education necessary to prepare for a higher place in the life to come. That is what your teachers have taught you, haven't they?"

"Yes, father."

"Then we have no hesitation about choosing the harder path when it is offered, if that is the direction in which our duty lies, do we?"

"No, father."

"But when there is a conflict of loyalties, decisions are sometimes difficult. I'm not speaking about myself now—the direction in which my duty lies is clear. But in your case you have two paths to choose from. If you go with your mother when she returns with the little ones to her parents, you will be responsible for her welfare and your path will not be an easy one. If you decide to go with me, the path almost certainly leads to death, but hopefully death with honor. This is what you must decide for yourself. I think you have reached the age when you can make up your own mind. It is a choice I cannot make for you."

For Chikara, this was a moment he had been waiting for and he had prepared his answer long ago. Without hesitation he replied, "I will go with you father. I know why you are sending mother away—to protect her. If I went with her I would only be protecting myself and that is not the act of a man—of a samurai."

Oishi was pleased at his son's response and felt pride in his heritage. It was true that the blossoms of today draw strength from the roots of a thousand years ago. Still he did not want to rush the boy into any hasty decision and urged him to consider carefully what he was doing.

"I already have," the boy assured him. "I am a man and must go with the men. Any other path would be cowardly."

Oishi smiled and took the boy by the hand. "Welcome to our band," he said. "From now on your responsibilities will be equal to those of any of us."

Chikara smiled back at him. He had finally gotten what he wanted more than anything else in the world, and as he left his father his eyes were shining and his chest was puffed out with pride.

Within a day the rest of the family was packed and ready to leave and Oishi saw them off with a stern expression to hide his true feelings. The small children's wide eyes were red from crying but in their father's presence they stifled their sobs. Mimura accompanied them, leading the pack horse that carried their belongings, but he would return as soon as they were located in their home. As they went out the gate, Oishi's wife turned for one last look at her husband, wavered for a moment, and then hurried on. Both of them knew they would never meet again.

Chapter Eleven

OF THE THREE LARGE PLEASURE QUARTERS in Kyoto, Gion was by far the most popular. And of all the geisha houses in Gion, the one that enjoyed the most enviable reputation for the quality of its services was the Flying Crane. The proprietor, a shrewd, perspiring hulk of a man named Hoshino, had worked hard to make his place the best in Kyoto, and he meant to keep it that way. Good service paid off in profits and Hoshino would do anything to make money.

At the moment he was worried about the party in one of the rooms overlooking the river. Two of the guests he knew by sight, a couple of local fellows named Shindo and Koyama. But the other two samurai were obviously inside a geisha house for the first time and did not seem to know how to relax and enjoy themselves. The one with the high forehead was especially ill at ease, and Hoshino feared he might be a man of influence who would carry away the impression that the Flying Crane was a dull place.

Hoshino stood in the hallway outside and perspired in recurrent gushes as the conversation beyond the paper door lagged to the point where he could stand no more. This called for drastic measures and he raised a damp arm to summon a passing waitress.

"Get Okaru," he said, and the girl bowed quickly and went to do as she was told.

In the room within, Oishi was indeed bored.

The teahouse was picturesque, and he was sure this room overlooking the sunny Kamo River was the best in the house, but the endless chatter of the geisha at his side was more than he had bargained for.

There were four of them, one for each of the guests, and all had brought in lacquered trays holding saké bottles and cups. They were dressed in bright kimono of the richest imaginable materials, with wide contrasting obi tied in huge bows. Their faces were painted white and lip rouge was applied to their lower lips. Over it all their hair was done in an elaborate piled-up style and decorated with hair ornaments.

The girls had introduced themselves with an engaging informality and laughingly applied nicknames to all four. Oishi was simply called "Uncle," Shindo was "Mr. Fox," Koyama was "Mr. Mouse," and Kataoka, of course, became "Mr. Monkey." Drinks were poured, toasts were made, the cups were drained and filled again, but while Shindo and Koyama, and even to some extent Kataoka, began to enjoy themselves, Oishi found it impossible to join in. The girl by his side was young enough to be his daughter and he felt foolish drinking with her. He had almost made up his mind to leave when there was an unexpected development.

He had turned aside to mutter some comment to Kataoka when the girl between them got up to go for a food tray. He was dimly aware that the other girls left at the same time but seemingly all returned together with colorful and appetizing dishes that were plainly concocted with no regard for the Shogun's edict prohibiting the eating of meat or fish.

Oishi turned directly to his own tray when it was placed before him and did not realize that it was now a different geisha kneeling at his side. It was the unaccustomed silence from her direction that finally caused him to turn to her. When he did so, he quickly caught his breath. Close beside him, with a tranquil smile that put him at ease at once, was the most beautiful woman he had ever seen. This was Okaru, the number one geisha in the geisha capital of the world.

Her age was impossible to guess, although she was certainly no child. Her kimono was exquisite, but no more so than that of the other girls. Her face was distinguished mainly by a high-bridged and aristocratic nose, but it was her eyes that captured Oishi's attention most of all. They were large and clear, with a depth to their expression that immediately set her apart from the other bland-faced girls of the quarter.

In a low musical voice she explained what the various dishes on his tray were and showed him the right way to eat them. Later, as the other geisha danced and sang, she explained the words and movements so that he could fully appreciate them.

Then she rose to dance herself and Oishi was captivated by her grace. To the solo plunking of a sensual samisen she posed and gestured in a simple story of flirtation and unrequited love that required no translation.

Later the other girls danced again and finally Shindo and Koyama, both quite tipsy, did a comic dance together that was a burlesque of the girls' movements. Oishi laughed aloud for the first time and the atmosphere of the party became much more relaxed.

When the time came to leave, they were escorted outside to the gate by the geisha and by Hoshino himself. Here, in exaggerated sorrow at parting, the girls bowed low and begged the men to come again. Assurances were freely given, but Oishi, who had not taken his eyes off Okaru all evening, was undoubtedly the most sincere. It had been a night he would never forget.

From every standpoint, Oishi's first visit to Gion was a success. People began to talk about his surprising turn to dissipation, which was exactly what he wanted them to do. The more talk, the more his reputation would be slandered and the less menacing he would be considered as a threat to Kira. The geisha houses became his constant habitat, as he labored to ruin what had always been most precious to him.

Additional spies were soon required to keep up with his frenetic activities and he was pleased to see the trouble he was causing in the enemy camp. He was aware that he was also risking some confusion in his own ranks, but that was a chance he felt he had to take.

On a typical day he would rise late, eat a hasty meal, and immediately be off to town. Those who were unable or unwilling to rise when he did would join the party later, locating it by the presence outside of a spy disguised as a *komuso*. These spies soon became so familiar to them that Kataoka began calling them his "guides to the pleasure spots" to their hidden faces, and then laughing at their obvious embarrassment.

After an afternoon of drinking and the games which Oishi finally came to tolerate, they would usually move on to another establishment for dinner and sometimes to a third teahouse for after-dinner entertainment. It was in moving from one place to another, and particularly on the way home late at night, that they made the most of their situation. Oishi would drunkenly accost the passers-by and otherwise make an unruly spectacle of himself. When the weather was fine he would even take a group of geisha and hangers-on to a public place like

Gion Park and carry on a riotous picnic in full view of the respectable strata of society. The people of Kyoto were accustomed to fun-loving visitors, but Oishi went much too far in their eyes.

Disregarding the cost to his reputation, however, the plan seemed to be working. Week after week the reports went back to Edo that he was spending money like a fool and holding no meetings with his men that were not out-and-out drinking bouts. Kataoka was characterized as a court jester and Shindo and Koyama could certainly not be labeled mighty warriors in anybody's book. Naturally, along with such reports went additional bills for the extra spies required and the distraught Chisaka was finally driven to make an economy move. The spy force was arbitrarily cut back to Fujii and one helper, not to mention the cook who was still on duty at Yamashina. It was an impossible assignment for two men and they were rapidly driven to distraction by lack of sleep and Oishi's playful attempts to confuse them. The Ako group took to leaving by rear entrances, going and coming separately, and otherwise making the spies' assignment as difficult as possible. Fujii still wore the basket over his head so there was no direct confrontation, but it was obvious that the shoe was on the other foot and Oishi laughed to think that he had at last scored against his formidable enemy.

Unfortunately for Oishi, most of the conversation in the geisha houses centered around their own floating world of pleasure, including the theater and the popular actors and artists of the day. Of these matters he was completely ignorant, pleading that he was just a simple samurai from the country and had no experience in such things. It was late one afternoon at the Flying Crane, which Oishi seemed to visit more than any other geisha house, when yet another lively discussion arose about the relative merits of certain actors. Oishi excused himself to get some air when Okaru suggested brightly that he go see the Kabuki himself so that he would know what they were talking about. The other geisha present gasped at her impudence, but Oishi pretended not to notice.

He turned to Okaru and politely thanked her for the suggestion. He felt she might be making fun of him but he decided to play along and agreed to go to the theater the very next day. It had never occurred to him to visit a public theater, he said, and he might find it amusing. Behind his back Shindo and Koyama winked at each other to hear this; they were sure it was only the saké Oishi had drunk that was talking. He was not the sort of man to frequent public places willingly.

The party continued until quite late that night and when they were finally ready to leave Kataoka found only one basket-headed spy waiting at the entrance. He reported this to Oishi and they agreed that a little game was in order. After they said their farewells to the geisha and the proprietor, the men from Ako exchanged hats and outer clothing with Shindo and Koyama, who then walked silently out the gate. The spy dutifully followed them, and Oishi and Kataoka, watching from a balcony, exploded in a fit of laughter. Then, in their companions' clothes, they slipped quietly out the back way. Although Oishi was not aware of it and would have been quite concerned if he had known, there was an unseen observer of their antics. The geisha Okaru watched from an upstairs window with an expression of more than passing curiosity.

The next day, to everyone's surprise, Oishi announced that he was indeed going to the Kabuki theater. Shindo and Koyama, already fans of this new kind of theatrical, so much livelier than the stately Noh of the court, accepted his invitation with alacrity. Kataoka was not as enthusiastic; he had no more knowledge of such things than his leader, but he had no intention of letting him jostle with the common people unattended and went along to act as bodyguard.

The first performance of the day began at noon, but Oishi insisted on stopping off at a teahouse for saké on the way and they missed it. As the afternoon went on, Shindo warned that they had better get there in time for the second performance or all the seats would be gone, but Oishi ignored him and poured another drink. For the scheme he had in mind he needed some fortification, and when he was finally ready to go it was quite late in the afternoon.

As Shindo had feared, the theater was sold out by the time they got there. As they arrived at the theater they could see would-be customers being turned away. Oishi, however, in a tipsy and not very happy frame of mind, decided that they were going to get in anyway and called for the manager. When that apprehensive gentleman appeared Oishi threatened to throw him into the adjoining Kamo River if he did not make a place for them immediately. The manager mopped his bald head and promised to see what he could do and after a short wait they were escorted inside by an usher.

As they went down the narrow aisle in the semi-darkened theater, Oishi could see that the mat-covered floor was divided by low railings into boxes which were jammed with customers of all ages and social standings. In order to seat Oishi, the manager had to evict four merchants from a choice box in the center of the hall who were now eyeing the newcomers with ill-concealed annoyance as they retrieved their lunch boxes and started up the aisle. Oishi noisily directed his companions to their places and peered around the theater, pointing to the side boxes in the balconies and wondering aloud if they were better seats. He could see that the merchant and geisha class were well represented and there were even a few samurai, or ronin, including one huge fellow with some cohorts in the adjoining box. In spite of the fact that the play was in progress Oishi now turned to opening the saké they had brought with them and caused additional confusion as he called for the manager to bring hot water to heat it in. No one, of course, was bold enough to remonstrate with him, although the big samurai in the next box was plainly annoyed. He was far from sober himself, but he was trying to follow the play and he grumbled at Oishi's lack of manners.

Oishi disregarded him completely and only when he finally got his warm saké did he give his attention to what was happening on the stage. When he was able to focus, he saw that the setting represented an ordinary peasant's cottage and that the performers, all men, were dressed in ordinary peasants' clothes. This he found most dull; after all, the fields were full of peasants and you did not have to come to the theater to look at them. What he found strange was that they were not talking like any peasants he had ever heard, but were delivering their lines in a highly stylized manner that seemed to him anything but lifelike. The noble sentiments they expressed seemed out of place for such rude characters and he found it hard to believe that the audience would actually accept such stuff. As he listened more closely he was amazed to find that the characters were discussing such things as Confucian ethics and the choice between duty to one's superior or humanity toward those one loved. To Oishi it was absurd that they should appreciate such weighty matters and he dug Kataoka in the ribs and made a slighting remark about the exalted peasants they were having the pleasure of meeting.

Kataoka laughed loudly and the others with Oishi joined in. The samurai in the next box glowered more deeply and muttered to his companions. He was beginning to get a little tired of these interruptions.

Now the heroine of the play appeared. She was a "lady" of noble birth and Oishi was immediately incensed that the players would have the temerity to portray someone of higher rank than themselves. Furthermore, it appeared that she had been badly treated by her husband and taken a lover among the merchant class. She had fled her home and was waiting to meet him at the peasant's hut, but Oishi never let the meeting take place.

Angrily he rose and shouted that the actor was a fake, that he had no concept of how to play a noble woman who would never behave in such a disgusting manner in the first place, and demanded that the show be stopped. There was a shocked silence for a moment, on stage and off, and then the samurai in the next box jumped up, exasperated beyond all endurance.

"Shut up, you ignorant son of a beast!" he shouted at Oishi. "You show less good manners than the townspeople—and this is not the first time you've made a fool of yourself in Kyoto from what I hear!"

Oishi was startled for a moment, then with a curse he quickly grabbed for his sword. It seemed to be stuck in its scabbard, and the other samurai stopped his glowering to laugh loudly and derisively.

"The sword once worn is now for kitchen use, eh?" He laughed again and turned to his companions. "Look, he calls himself a samurai, better than those on the stage or in the audience, and he carries a rusty sword!" He laughed again and this time Oishi made a vicious cut at his legs with the sword still in its scabbard. The big man tried to leap out of the way and fell over one of the low partitions between the boxes. He landed on top of another paying customer, an old woman who cursed at him like a laborer, and he got up to face the laughter of Oishi's drunken companions. The hands of the big man's own followers went to their swords but he motioned them back. He stared for a moment at the ludicrous spectacle of Oishi, sword at the ready but still in its scabbard, and then threw back his head and laughed. He grabbed his own sword and raised it high, and it was seen that it, too, was safely sheathed in its scabbard. With a mock cry of attack he lunged fiercely at Oishi and missed him to crash into another partition.

The spectators around them quickly gave way as they saw that it was turning into a full-scale battle and both Oishi's men and those of his opponent formed semicircles behind their leaders to keep anyone from interfering.

The circling and slashing of the swordsmanship contest continued, never so strangely out of place as on the floor of a darkened theater with the partitions between the boxes serving as obstacles. Both men were apparently in poor physical condition, besides being drunk, and the townspeople found it a noisy, odious performance. Many of them began to leave the theater, in deep resentment that men of this station should come into a theater and break up the show. As busy as he was, Oishi sensed this and felt greatly embarrassed, even though his predicament was all of his own making.

He endeavored to bring the fight to a quick close but his opponent was just as handy as he, and the silly circling and slashing went on. Never in his life had Oishi felt or looked so foolish, and he cursed himself for getting involved in such a scrape. Realizing that he could not look any worse if he tried, he deliberately tripped himself and fell flat on his face before his opponent. The big man whooped in victory and tapped him not too lightly on the head with his sheathed sword in a gesture of victory. Oishi drew himself to his knees and made a mock bow of surrender, and the big man laughed and withdrew to his own box.

The skylights were opened by now and the performance was at an end. Some members of the audience were still in their places, hoping that the play would begin again, but most had left out of fear or disgust. The big samurai ordered his men to pick up their things and prepare to leave and Oishi was about to do the same when he happened to look around at the boxes on the side again and saw Okaru. She was sitting there talking with a little *maiko*, or apprentice geisha, and Oishi could not be sure whether she had seen his performance or not. He assumed she had, however, and turned away in regret and embarrassment. Shindo noticed this, as drunk as he was, and called it to Koyama's attention. When Koyama finally understood what Shindo was trying to tell him they exchanged a knowing glance.

Oishi abruptly left the theater, his little group following, with Shindo and Koyama bowing in recognition to Okaru who politely nodded in return. Oishi missed this interchange; he was still thinking about his own disgraceful behavior. In his mind there was only one cause for satisfaction about the whole episode; if any of Kira's spies had been watching they had certainly received proof that the object of their surveillance was a complete fool. His sword was evidently rusty, his swordsmanship was appallingly bad, and he had no more thought for his reputation than a street beggar.

In disgust with himself and to deliberately compound the injury to his reputation, Oishi insisted they stop at the first "teahouse" they came to, even though it was a low-class establishment that he would ordinarily have shunned. Dejectedly he slumped down just inside the door and demanded service of the watch-girl. Here he consumed more saké, which was not the best, served by "geisha" who were not the best either. These girls were straight off the farms with no training in the social graces whatsoever. Their function was to serve saké and sleep with the customers when requested; their abilities to entertain in other ways were strictly limited. Oishi listened in boredom as they chattered among themselves in their local dialects, all of which grated unpleasantly on his ear. But he was there to drink, not to talk, and he devoted himself single-mindedly to that purpose.

Hours later Shindo and Koyama had quietly slipped away and Oishi was left lying in a stupor with his head cradled in the lap of the watch-girl, who was crooning a folk song of home in a wavering monotone. Kataoka had fallen asleep in the corner, exhausted and out of patience with his leader.

Suddenly there was a commotion at the front door and the

girl paused to look up blearily. Oishi raised himself to listen, then sank back again against her as she resumed her song. The next thing Oishi knew, the door was thrown open with a bang and Hara, his eyes blazing, stood in the doorway. Oishi tried to pull himself up but his hand slipped and he went crashing back against the girl, who was stunned into silence at the sight of the wild-eyed samurai before them.

"Hara," Oishi said thickly as he got to his knees. "Welcome, old friend... Kataoka, looks who's here—it's our old friend Hara."

Kataoka roused himself sleepily, but when he saw who it was in the doorway he sat up with a start. He was about to say something to Hara by way of explanation but the look on the other's face stopped him. He had never seen such an expression of fury on Hara's face before and for once he was at a loss for words.

"So the stories were true!" Hara hissed at them, his hands trembling at his two swords as though he would like to put them to use. "I never would have believed it of either of you so I had to come and see for myself. And you, Oishi, were so upset when I sank to becoming an archery instructor!"

Oishi rose unsteadily to his feet. "Now just a minute, old friend..."

"I'm not your friend," Hara interrupted him icily. "You're a disgrace to the name of 'samurai.'" He shook his head. "I would never have guessed that you would willingly wallow in such filth as this!"

"Now wait a minute!" Kataoka said angrily, but Hara was not about to wait for anyone.

"Who pays for all this whoring, Oishi-dono!" he asked with a rising note of fury in his voice. "While some of our men are starving in the streets, by what right do you spend our funds in this way?"

"Hara, you've said enough!" Oishi shouted.

"I have said enough. I'm through talking to you and I'm through listening, too. I'm going to spread the word to all our band that Oishi has become a thief and a rake and is not to be trusted. I should cut both of you down and be done with it!"

He turned to go out the door and Kataoka flung himself desperately after him.

"Hara, don't you see..." he began, but Hara, in a supremely insulting gesture, placed his foot squarely in Kataoka's chest and pushed him violently backward.

"Son of a beast!" he spat through clenched teeth, and then he stepped out through the doorway.

As he closed the door, Oishi glimpsed a young man waiting behind him but the face was not familiar and he was quickly forgotten.

Hara was gone and Oishi and Kataoka were left sadly shaking their heads.

After a moment the girl, still white and shaking, began to edge toward the inner entrance to the teahouse, but Oishi saw her out of the corner of his eye. He moved to block her path and forced a smile to his lips.

"Please," he said, "it's nothing to be alarmed about. Our friend is very old fashioned and doesn't understand why we like to have a good time once in a while."

The girl hesitated and the color gradually came back to her cheeks.

"It's too late for singing now but we really appreciate the fine time you showed us." He opened his purse and took out a few coins, which he dropped from one hand into the other as he continued. "You'll forgive us, won't you? And not mention this episode to anyone?"

The girl took a deep breath when she saw the money, and when he finished and handed it to her she smiled and revealed her crooked teeth.

"Thank you, sir. Please come again."

Oishi and Kataoka bowed clumsily to her and left. Out in the air Kataoka moved apart by himself and for once had no lighthearted comment to make. Oishi realized how deeply his old friend had been humiliated by the afternoon's happenings, and wondered if Hara, too, had lost all faith in his leader. Under the circumstances he could not blame either of them if they had, and when they reached Yamashina Oishi went to bed in a black and all but hopeless mood.

Chapter Twelve

IN THE MIDDLE OF THE NIGHT Oishi was half-awakened by whispered voices in the corridor outside his room. He tried to make out what they were saying but the sounds blurred in his head and he rolled over to go back to sleep. Facing away from the doorway he imagined he heard someone softly open and close the *shoji*, but he was too miserable and drunk to care and tightly closed his eyes until he fell asleep again.

It was some time later when he happened to turn toward the door that he sensed that someone was in the room. And not only in the room but in the same bed with him! There was a dim form lying on the mattress next to him, and he raised up on his arm with an exclamation.

His first thought was that it was his wife, returned from her parents' home without permission, and he felt a simultaneous urge to embrace her and to strike her for her disobedience. Then the figure turned more directly toward him and he saw by the moonlight that filtered milky-white through the paper windows that it was Okaru. Again his impulses were contradictory. He knew instantly that her being there was the doing of Shindo and Koyama, and this made him angry and resentful.

But on the other hand the whole thing was funny! It was a cruel joke to try to get him involved with a "substitute wife," and he could not help chuckling in a kind of mirthless despair. At the sound the girl looked at him curiously. He could see now how pale her skin was and could distinguish a faint reddish glow through her dark perfumed hair. She was beautiful, he had to admit, and he moved closer as she watched him, motionless.

He reached out to touch her to make sure she was real and felt a surge of passion as he felt the warm skin of her cheek. His hand moved to the back of her neck and he stroked it softly under her low collar. Then his hand moved to her throat and then slowly down the front of her flimsy kimono, opening it all the way.

Abruptly he opened it wider, first one side and then the other, until she lay fully revealed in the pale light. Her skin was so smooth, so perfect, that he hesitated to touch it again. Then he placed his palm on her chest and felt her quickening heartbeat.

After all, he thought, she did not have to be here if she did not want to be. She was of first-class rank and could refuse unwanted bed partners. And was it not truly a shame for a man not to eat a meal set before him?

With a sigh he rolled heavily onto her, but the night was not yet through with surprises. As her yielding body received him, he felt a sensation such as he had never known before.

Deep inside her he felt a rhythmic throbbing that caressed him unceasingly until he reached the point of ecstasy. Then it continued so that he felt exquisite pain as he was drained of every drop of passion. Was it a trick, he wondered, as he rolled off her? Was it a technique she had learned in the geisha house, or was it some rare gift she had been born with? But he lacked the courage to ask her. Leave well enough alone, he thought, and quickly fell asleep.

In the morning when he woke and found the girl still beside him, he felt thoroughly ashamed of his behavior. He saw that she was already awake and he spoke to her in apology.

"There should be no intimacy without politeness."

She smiled at him for the first time and he was again aware of her beauty. There was a perpetual melancholy expression in her eyes that gave even her simple smile a touch of mystery.

"It is a matter of no great importance," she said simply.

Oishi was reassured and grateful for a moment but then his mind went back to the brawl in the theater. She had been there and surely she must have a low opinion of him for his silly antics in a theater full of people. Now another thought occurred to him. Since she had seen him and must think him a fool, why had she consented to move in with him when his well-meaning relatives had sought her out? Did she need the money they were undoubtedly paying her? Not likely, for one of her class. Could it be that she was a spy herself, cleverly gotten into his house through Shindo's or Koyama's gullibility?

She must have guessed what he was thinking, but as she smiled at him again he took refuge in the banter of the tea-house.

"A woman who has a smile for everybody is coldhearted, they say."

"That may be," she agreed, still smiling. "But what makes you think I smile for everyone?"

"It is your business to do so," he said simply. "I don't flatter myself that I'm any different from the rest."

"All men are different and yet all are the same."

"True," he agreed. "But some men are to be avoided, not sought out. Troublemakers and the like can bring nothing but pain to those around them."

"Sleeve touches sleeve because it was predestined in the former world," she said quietly.

"And what is joined must separate," he said, just as softly. Then he abruptly changed the subject, rather than risk going too far in a discussion of themselves.

"The Kabuki was not what you said it would be," he began, falling back on the subject they had discussed before.

"I'm sorry you didn't enjoy it," she answered, readily changing with him to a lighter conversational tone.

"You said it was realistic—to me it was just the opposite. Peasants don't behave like that—and neither do noblewomen."

Okaru's eyebrows raised slightly but she remained silent.

"No samurai's wife would leave him for a commoner like that fellow in the play," he went on. "It was completely unbelievable. I can see how ignorant people who don't know any better might be taken in by it, but anyone who has been around the nobility at all would know that such things don't happen."

"I'm sure you've known more noblewomen than I have," she admitted. "But you didn't see the end of the play. The young commoner turns out to be a samurai himself! And even if you didn't guess it, most of the people in the audience knew it because they'd seen the play before."

Oishi was silent for a moment. "Well, that might make some difference," he said grudgingly at last. "But that still doesn't justify her infidelity."

"But what if her husband had treated her cruelly? What if he had divorced her for some trivial reason and she had no one to turn to?"

This conversation, too, was beginning to hit uncomfortably close to home and Oishi hesitated. "Perhaps," he said weakly. "But still no decent woman would throw herself so promiscuously at a man."

Now it was Okaru's turn to feel uncomfortable but she merely nodded in agreement. "Yes," she said. "You are probably right. I haven't known many noblewomen—many decent women—and I'm sure you're right about the way they behave."

Oishi realized too late how his remark had stung her, but he could find no words of apology that seemed adequate. In his embarrassment he fell back on his customary blunt manner.

"What are you doing here?" he asked.

"Your relatives asked me to come," she said simply. "They said you needed a woman in the house so that you wouldn't chase around the pleasure quarters every night and ruin your health."

"They came to you? They sought you out?" he asked.

"Yes, of course," she said in surprise. "Did you think that I?..." She hesitated, then smiled. "Not that a woman doesn't need a man as much as he needs her."

Oishi's thoughts were still on Shindo and Koyama and he only dimly heard her. Was concern over his health their true motive? Or was there something else they hoped to gain by bringing the girl into the house? They certainly must have been watching him carefully to know that this girl of all the geisha in Kyoto had attracted him the most. But what would happen if he let himself become too involved with her? Was that also part of their plan? With a puzzled sigh, he turned back to the girl.

"What about your other customers, girl? Can you afford to devote yourself to one at the expense of the others?"

"That's my business," she said with a laugh.

"But why pick a dissolute old man like me?"

"I'll tell you a secret, old man," she said mysteriously. "You're not that many years older than I am."

Oishi nodded. "Perhaps that's why you're more attractive to me than the rest—I mean..." He stopped, flustered, aware that he had said more than he meant to. He waited for her to laugh at his slip but she merely waited for him to finish.

"I mean that young girls are foolish. But so are men when they reach my age."

"But not you."

"How can you say that?" he asked in astonishment. "I'm the biggest buffoon in Kyoto. You saw a sample of my behavior in the theater yesterday."

"Just as I don't think you are so old, I don't think you are so silly," she said matter-of-factly.

"What *do* you see in me?" he asked, raising his voice in exasperation.

"Perhaps I see someone who has suffered from a loss of position and I sympathize with him."

"Sympathize or pity?" he asked cuttingly.

"Oh, I don't pity you. I feel that someday you will regain what is rightfully yours. As you know, a man is in a better position to do that than a woman is."

Oishi stared at her. She seemed to be telling him quite frankly that she knew all about him. Or was this merely the manner of the geisha, a smile and a soothing word for everyone?

"You're talking nonsense," he told her. "What I've lost can never be regained—and all the determination in the world won't help get it back."

"Whatever you say," she smilingly agreed.

"You saw me at the theater," he said in a weary voice. "You still think that after that disgraceful exhibition that I am a fighter."

"If necessary," she nodded, "I think you could be."

"And what leads you to that conclusion?"

"Just from what I know of you, in the few times we've met. For example, I have an idea that things went pretty much as you wanted them to in the theater."

Oishi was startled. "What do you mean?"

For an answer she got up out of the bed and moved toward the corner where he had thrown his sword the night before.

"I've made a bet with myself about your sword," she said, picking it up in its scabbard. Oishi made an involuntary move to stop her, then quietly lay back to see what she would do. "I've bet that it's not as rusty as you pretend."

She moved back to stand over him in her flimsy nightdress, her hand on the hilt of the sword. "Am I right?"

He stared at her, realizing that there was nothing he could say to stop her.

"Am I right?" she repeated, and then effortlessly drew the shiny blade out of its scabbard to hold it raised high over her head in a mock gesture of attack.

Oishi merely grunted and continued to stare. Suddenly she broke into a peal of laughter and returned the sword to its scabbard. She let it drop to the floor and stood there, continuing to laugh in triumph and relief that she had been right.

Oishi's face broke into a smile and then he began to laugh, too. Stealthily he moved his foot to hook behind her leg. He pulled gently behind her knee and she let herself be pulled down on top of him. If she were a spy, he was thinking—but his thoughts were interrupted by her round hot mouth on his and he gave himself to her as she desired. It cannot be denied that a charred post is easily set afire.

Chapter Thirteen

IN THE ARCHERY SHOP IN OSAKA, Hara was greatly disturbed. His hands trembled as he lifted a bow and notched an arrow, and his aim was so bad that he missed the cloth target altogether.

Under his breath he cursed. Never in his life had he been so upset about anything. Even moving out of the castle at Ako had not robbed him of his faith in eventual justice as much as had his encounter with Oishi.

Hara was an uncomplicated man and could only believe what he could see. He felt defiled and insulted by Oishi's actions and even reproached himself for not killing his leader on the spot. In spite of their long friendship, there were limits to what a samurai could endure.

Fortunately he was alone at the moment and no one could see his bad marksmanship. He would have to get a better grip on himself before any of the townspeople came for their lessons. His temper was so frayed since returning from Kyoto that their clumsiness was bound to irritate him even more than usual.

In fact, he reflected, he had had only one really promising student since he opened shop. Of course, the school was only a front, but he derived some satisfaction from having gotten the rudiments of archery over to one muscular young man. This smiling fellow was named Konishi and he had become Hara's assistant and almost constant companion. He expressed great admiration for Hara's prowess with a bow and begged for stories about the castle life in Ako. He said he was the son of a merchant and had never personally known any samurai before.

This show of interest was flattering and Hara took extra pains with his lessons. He reflected that if the young man continued to show progress he might even speak to Oishi about finding some way for him to help with their enterprise. But then he recalled his last meeting with Oishi and snorted angrily. He would never ask Oishi for anything again. When it came to the matter of revenge, he would take it himself if needs be.

His thoughts were interrupted by Konishi's noisy arrival. The young man ran in breathlessly and bowed low in a swift movement that took his knees and head to the floor in one continuous movement.

"Hey! What's the matter now?" Hara asked roughly.

Konishi raised his head and grinned. "Sensei," he said, addressing Hara with the honorific term of teacher, "You'll never guess who I saw in Osaka today!"

"I'm in no mood for guessing games," Hara said, turning away.

"One of your countrymen!" the young man went on excitedly and Hara turned back to face him.

"Someone from Ako?"

"Yes, he's in business here and seems to be doing quite well."

"In business? Who could that be? Did you learn his name?"

"Oh no. I only recognized the crest of Ako on his place of business."

"Mmm. And what kind of business was it? Not another archery school?"

"No, sensei. It was a dry goods store—quite a large one."

"Dry goods?...Who could that be?..."

Hara mused for a moment, then abruptly started out of the shop.

"Come on," he said roughly. "Show me where you saw the crest of Asano on a dry goods store."

Konishi scrambled to his feet and with a smile followed him out.

It was only a short walk through the bustling streets of Osaka to the store that had so excited Konishi. When they reached it, he pointed and grinned, and Hara, until now not convinced that the boy was telling a straight story, winced in spite of himself. Sure enough, there before an ordinary dry goods store, in plain view of all the passers-by, was the Asano crest, displayed like a sign advertising noodles or rice.

Hara gritted his teeth and started forward, the boy following. In spite of his preoccupation, Hara knew that he should not involve his young assistant in clan affairs and gruffly ordered him to wait outside. Then he marched on into the store.

Inside, he looked around for some clue to the owner's identity but found nothing. There were bolts of cloth being displayed to customers by several young salesmen but Hara did not recognize any of them. Then he heard a familiar voice and looked around. Coming out of a back room with some special goods for display was the old treasurer of the Asano clan, Ono!

Hara was momentarily surprised, but then he realized that he had no reason to be. Ono was the kind who would think nothing of rubbing the family crest in the dirt if it would help him get ahead. Whether the money he had used to go into business was gained by honest means or not, Hara had no way of knowing. But he did have some ideas about Ono's present affluence and some uses that could be made of it.

He stepped forward and grabbed Ono roughly by the collar.

"Please," he said to the old man, whose face had turned suddenly white, "show me some of your special wares."

He pushed Ono back the way he had come, back into a storeroom where they could talk alone. He rested the old man on a roll of material and folded his arms as he stood in front of him.

"I must congratulate you, Ono-san, on your prosperity. You must be doing better than any of the ronin of Ako."

There was no hint of a threat in his voice but Ono was not fooled. He knew perfectly well where he stood in Hara's eyes.

"Now just a minute, old friend, there's nothing wrong with what I've done..."

"Did I say there was?" Hara asked innocently. "I think you've done remarkable things with the small amount of pension we all received. I always knew that you had a feel for money—now I can see that you know how to make it increase as well."

"I've worked hard here, my friend," Ono said defensively. "My son and I have put in long hours to make this a going concern."

"And you deserve every credit," Hara said, nodding in agreement.

Ono shifted uneasily. There was something coming that he was sure he would not like, but he still could not quite fathom Hara's intentions. There was one stratagem that always worked, however, and he decided the time had come to use it.

"I'm sorry if things have been hard for you," he said with a sickly grin. "I've noticed that you have few customers at your archery school. I've meant to stop in several times, but as I say, there's always the press of business..."

Hara said nothing, so he continued.

"As a matter of fact I was saying to my son just the other day, 'Why not ask Hara to come in with us? He'd be a good worker and I'm sure he could use the extra money.'"

Hara continued to regard him without expression and Ono talked a little faster.

"Could I help you out now, old friend? Perhaps a loan..."

The old man scrambled to his feet and hurried to a corner of the room to dig out a cash box from under a pile of goods.

"See! This is the reward for sound investment of capital and labor. Take as much as you need! I'll just make a note of the amount and..."

Hara calmly walked over and took the box in one huge hand. He had found the perfect solution for replenishing the coffers that Oishi was robbing. Without another word he started to walk out of the store while Ono gaped after him like a dying fish.

"But no—not all. You can't do this..."

Hara stopped and turned to him.

"It's for a worthy cause, not for my use. You'll be glad you made such a fine contribution."

He started out, then turned again.

"And take down the Asano crest you have hanging outside, will you?" he said politely. "If you don't, I'll come back and take a sword to you as you deserve."

Ono continued to stare after him as he left. Then he kicked a bolt of material with a savage curse. He had been robbed in his own store and there was nothing he could do about it.

On the way out, Hara bumped into Ono's son coming in. One glance at the cash box told the young man all he needed to know and he hurried past Hara with a quick bow. Hara snorted. The boy had no more spine than his father. The clan was well rid of both of them.

Outside he rejoined Konishi, who was dying with curiosity about what had happened in the store, but Hara said nothing.

Resolutely he strode though the dust-filled street, emptying of shoppers now in the late day, back to the archery shop where he could count the money undisturbed. He had very specific plans for the use of these funds and none of them included his old leader, Oishi. Tonight he would write to Horibe and start things rolling toward what those followers with real courage desired most.

Chapter Fourteen

ONE MORNING OKARU WAS SURPRISED to receive a messenger with a note from her old employer, the proprietor of the Flying Crane. In it, Hoshino stated that he would be paying her a call that day if she had no objection. Oishi was out and she was alone in the house, except for Chikara and the little *maiko* she had brought to live with her. She saw no harm in the request for a meeting, and sent a note of acceptance back to him, although she had thought her ties with the Flying Crane was severed.

Okaru had an odd background for a geisha, although her little *maiko* was the only one with whom she ever discussed it. She was the daughter of a farmer who had been forced off his land by the consequences of the Life Preservation Laws. To support his family he had taken the shameful step of going into business, thereby dropping two steps down the social ladder of samurai, farmer, artisan, and merchant. Last, of course, came the *eta*, but they didn't really count in the social structure at all.

For a time things were not easy for her father in his new line of work, but then things began to go *too* well and that was his downfall. He became so successful in business that he foolishly began to spend his money on fancy clothes and other items more suitable for those of noble descent, at least in the eyes of the nobles. His expenditures came to the attention of the city governors and they in turn reported the matter to Edo. Almost immediately a message came from the Shogun in the form of an order to her father. He was to contribute "voluntarily" the funds necessary to erect a new Buddhist temple in the ever expanding suburbs of Osaka. He had no choice but to obey and the subsequent cost of materials and labor took every last cent of his fortune, just as the Shogun had planned. So he ended up where he had started, penniless, feeling himself more disgraced than ever, and lacking the spirit to try again. He died not long after his money was gone and his wife followed him within weeks. With a younger brother to support, Okaru was fortunately able to make use of her education in the graceful arts and had become a geisha.

She had not minded her life at the Flying Crane—anything was better than starving—and by devoting herself assiduously to the more difficult customers, she gained a reputation for herself as an expert soother of sorrows. Her employer recognized her value and gave her special privileges, but she was on such good terms with the other geisha that they were not jealous. Hoshino had hated to lose her, but the offer from Shindo and Koyama to buy her freedom was a generous one, and besides it coincided with Okaru's own wishes.

From their first meeting she had been attracted to Oishi, although she could not have said why. Perhaps it was the fact that he had lost something dear, yet had not given up hope of getting it back again that gave them something in common. She had been through such a heartbreaking experience herself and now saw an opportunity to help him. At any rate, she had not hesitated long when invited to join his household. She did not know until later that it was not Oishi's own idea for her to come live with him, but fortunately that had worked out all right, too. Now that she was there, she knew she would never leave voluntarily and she hoped he would never leave her. But it was only a small hope, for Okaru was a feeling, intelligent girl and for her it was plain to see that he was a man with a mission. The most she could ask for was to help him accomplish it.

But she wondered what it was Hoshino wanted. Did he miss her services and want her back? It was unusual for a girl to return to the gay quarters once she had left. And it was next to impossible for a first-class geisha to ever resume that position after she had spurned all her regular customers to go and live with one man.

Hoshino arrived on schedule, fat and panting and leaving a trail of steam. Strangely, he was alone, although he usually traveled with a retinue of servants or a footman at the very least. He laboriously climbed down out of the palanquin and entered the house.

"Ah, Okaru!" he called out in admiration and longing when he saw her. He had forgotten just how lovely she was and regretted more than ever that he had sold her away. She bowed low in greeting and then they went on into the house.

Kataoka arrived back at Yamashina before anyone else that evening. He had made another trip to Osaka to try to reason with Hara but it had been as fruitless as ever. He was surprised to see the palanquin waiting in front of the house and was about to check on its ownership when he saw someone coming out of the house and paused in the shadow of the wall.

He was perturbed at the sight of the fat Hoshino and tried to imagine some reason for such a visit. He drew a blank, however, and this troubled him. By moving in with Oishi, Okaru had cut herself free from the Flying Crane and it was presumptuous of Hoshino to try to re-establish their relationship. Kataoka was more than a little annoyed, besides being puzzled, and decided to follow the palanquin to see where it would go next. A little spying of his own might be profitable, he thought, and he took care to keep out of sight of the *komuso* across from the house.

Hoshino's path led straight back to the geisha house and Kataoka was about to return to Yamashina in disappointment when he saw that two men were waiting in an outer garden for the fat proprietor's return. They went up to him immediately and Kataoka could see that their discussion, whatever it was, was not on the most friendly terms. The two men kept their backs to the entrance, but Kataoka could see that Hoshino was bowing and begging for something, probably money. One of the two men roughly handed him a few coins and they abruptly withdrew, leaving him to wipe his face with an already damp rag.

Now the two men came closer to Kataoka and he stood quietly beside an ornamental wall outside the garden until they passed. When he could see their faces, he drew in his breath in sudden shock. One of the men was tall, thin, and deep voiced; it was none other than Fujii, the chief of the spies who had been following them for so many months! When they had gone by without noticing him, he quickly left the garden and hurried back to Yamashina.

"You slut!" he screamed, and hit her again the mouth.

Okaru's hand went to her face as she fell heavily back against the wall, but she uttered not a sound.

Kataoka grabbed her by the collar of her kimono and pulled her to him. Again he struck her and again she fell in silence. Blood was running from a corner of her mouth as she faced him with a pleading look in her eyes, but he paid no attention.

"How could you do such a thing—and to the man you say you love!"

He pulled her forward and was about to strike her with his clenched fist full in the face when the door behind him crashed opened and Oishi, his eyes blazing, took one long step into the room and seized Kataoka's arm.

"What are you doing to her? Have you gone mad?"

Kataoka tearfully sank to his knees.

"I wish I had gone mad. I wish I had not seen what I saw."

"What did you see?" Oishi demanded, still holding Kataoka's arm and staring in bewilderment at the disheveled Okaru.

"I would rather die than to have to tell you this—but she's a spy!"

Oishi dropped Kataoka's arm and took a step backward as though he was the one who had been struck. Okaru began to sob but if she was trying to say something, Oishi could not hear her.

He moved slowly toward the door, pausing only to mutter indistinctly. "Get out. Take your things and go."

Then he was gone and Kataoka continued to kneel, staring sightlessly at the floor. Okaru sobbed against the wall until her knees gave way and she sank to the floor with a half-crazed expression in her wide eyes.

It was Chikara who found her, late that night. He was awakened by a scream and dashed into the women's wing of the house. It was the little *maiko* who screamed but all she could do was point inside Okaru's room when Chikara appeared.

Okaru was hanging by her own scarf from a ceiling beam and Chikara, his eyes wide with dread, sprang forward to support her and to untie the knot. He lowered her to the floor and was listening for her heartbeat when she groaned faintly and he knew she was alive.

"Quickly," he told the little girl in the hallway. "Get my father."

"But I saw him," Kataoka was repeating. "He was the spy we've all been avoiding for all these months—Fujii. He was paying fat old Hoshino for his services directly after he had come from seeing Okaru. What else was I to think?"

"Be quiet," Oishi growled as he knelt beside the motionless form of his mistress, and tried to force some tea into her mouth. "I believe everything you say. But I should have listened to her side of it, too. Does this look like the act of a spy?" And he indicated the still form of the girl, the mark of the scarf still on her throat.

Kataoka was silent and they both watched Okaru anxiously. Chikara and the little *maiko* sat farther back in the room, careful to keep silent lest somebody notice them and send them to bed.

Okaru stirred and murmured something, then slowly opened her eyes. She looked around at them all, and then her eyes stopped on Oishi's face.

"I'm sorry," she said, in a formal tone of apology, and then the tears came to her eyes. "But I could not bear it when I saw your love for me die."

Oishi murmured something soothingly in her ear and a little smile came to her lips. Then he turned to the others.

"You can all go to bed now. Okaru is going to be all right."

Silently they all rose to go and Oishi and Okaru were left alone.

"He wanted me to spy—but I told him I could not do such a thing," she said painfully.

"I know—I know. Go to sleep now and tomorrow we'll have forgotten all about it."

He lay down beside her and, after a while, both of them slept.

Chapter Fifteen

IT WAS NOW THE TIME of the midsummer Ura Bon festival and Oishi decided it would do no harm to go all out in celebrating it. They had missed many holidays in the past year and now was the time to make up for them.

The house was decorated with paper lanterns, with braided paper birds that would whirl, rise and fall when ignited, and with vegetable decorations of welcome to the departed spirits. A special shrine was built just inside the entrance hall to O-Shoryo-sama, who represented the combined spirit of all their ancestors. The names of the departed were written on a long scroll and put inside the shrine, and incense was kept burning before it. Each of the living said their own prayers in their own way to the spirit, true to the tradition that one's own Buddha is the best to worship.

On the last morning of the Ura Bon the decorative food was loaded onto pampas-grass canoes and taken to the river. In the early dawn, candles were lit on the little boats which were then gently placed on the water and headed downstream. As they floated away, the watchers on the shore called their farewells to O-Shoryo-sama until the following year. Chikara and the little *maiko* were in charge of the boat launching and it was obvious that they were both enjoying themselves immensely. When the others had left, they stayed by the bank of the river and watched until the little lights disappeared down the river, and they began to feel the warmth of the rising sun.

"Where will we be when O-Shoryo-sama comes again, I wonder?" the little girl asked pensively as she lifted her head to the boy beside her.

"Who knows?" he answered lightly. "In this world, one step ahead is darkness."

"But wouldn't you like to know?" she asked. "Do you think we'll still be living here like we are now?"

"What's the difference? One place is like another, isn't it?"

"Oh, no," she said decisively. "No other place is as nice as this."

Chikara looked at her uncomfortably. He had no intention of giving away secrets but he felt he owed it to her not to give her any false hopes.

"What about the geisha house? Didn't you like it there?" he asked.

"Oh, yes. It was fun—part of the time. It was hard work, too, not that I minded that, but it was never...peaceful, the way it is here."

"I think it's too quiet here," said Chikara, somewhat belligerently. "When you're trained as a samurai, you've got to have a certain amount of action or you grow stale."

"I do miss some of the parties," she admitted, "but too many of those can get tiresome. If only I could work there part of the time and come here when I wanted to—then everything would be perfect."

"What do you do at the parties," he asked curiously. He had never been inside a geisha house in his life and knew he was not likely to enter one in the future either.

"Oh, you serve tea and saké, and smile. Mostly you try to learn from the first-class geisha like Okaru-san what pleases men the most. Then we have dancing and singing lessons and practice daily on the samisen so that when we come of age we'll be ready to be first-class geisha, too."

"And when will that be?"

"For me in two more years—I'll be sixteen then. That's the time I'm really looking forward to. Will you come and see me when I'm a geisha? Will you come to Gion? I'll be pleased to dance for you."

Chikara hesitated, then lied like a gentleman as he assured her that he would. Neither of them noticed that Oishi and Okaru had come back looking for them and now stood quietly on the bank above, smiling at their conversation.

"I'll be so glad to finish the training," the little girl went on. "Not that I'm not doing well," she added hastily. "Okaru says I'm very good for my age, but I get so cold in the winter sometimes when we have to sit still for long periods in a cold room."

"Do you have to do that, too?" asked Chikara. "I thought only samurai had to have that kind of training."

"Maybe being a samurai and being a geisha are not too different after all, do you think, Chikara-san?" she said with an air of great discovery.

"Oh, they're lots different," he protested. "Samurai have to learn to ride and to fight with swords and bows and arrows, and learn calligraphy and...lots of things that geisha don't."

"But we have to train our bodies and our minds strictly, too," she said. "I think they're something alike anyway."

"Well, maybe," he reluctantly agreed. "But don't tell anybody I said so."

On the bank Oishi smiled at Okaru and they moved quietly away. When they were back on the path that led to the house he spoke to her.

"And did you go through all that rigorous training, too? Even sitting in the cold room for hours without moving?"

She laughed. "I was spared much of that. I entered the profession late."

"I know," he said, and she looked at him in surprise.

"What do you know about me?" she asked.

"Everything—everything a curious monkey named Kataoka could find out."

She was silent for a moment, then spoke in a low voice.

"So you know what I meant when I said that I could sympathize with someone who had suffered a loss of position."

"But you've more than regained your position. A famous geisha is certainly of higher social rank than a merchant's daughter. And you did it all on your own and against great odds."

"As you will," she told him, suddenly deeply serious. "As you will."

Oishi knew now he had no secrets from this woman who thought so much as he did and he did not try to pretend with her any longer.

"You know that in the end you'll have to go back to the geisha house?" he said gently.

Okaru lifted her eyebrows. Evidently Oishi was unaware that such a move was not easy to arrange. And in her case it might prove to be impossible.

"Tomorrow blows tomorrow's wind," she said in a lighter tone. "I'll worry about that when the time comes."

"I hope you won't mind too much when the time does come."

"I've never regretted becoming a geisha," she told him. "Even now it has its advantages. When the autumn wind begins to blow in your heart and I become as useless as a paper fan, I will be able to make my own way as I would not if my station in life were different."

Oishi nodded. Okaru knew what she was doing and he respected her for her practicality. There was no point in denying that he would tire of her—she knew as well as he that that is not what would separate them.

They continued to walk slowly back to the house as the day became warmer and the cicadas began to hum. Oishi was reminded of the last meeting with his wife when he had given her the letter of divorce and he recalled her promise to pray for him. He hoped the faiths of both the women in his life would be justified. So much sacrifice had to be compensated for in the end.

When they reached the front of the house, Oishi, out of habit, checked to see if the spy was still across the way. There was a so-called *komuso* on duty as always and Oishi's forehead wrinkled as he muttered an oath under his breath.

Okaru's heart went out to him in sympathy. She knew what a strain he was under and especially how concerned he was about Hara, who continued to refuse to answer his messages. She tried to think of some way to help. What could be done to throw his enemies off her lover's trail once and for all? If she thought it would serve any purpose, she would pretend to be a spy and send out false messages. But if she were found out, suspicions would be aroused to such an extent that Oishi's position would be more difficult. So that was not a good plan.

She knew the spy force had been reduced since she had come to live at Yamashina, but merely reducing it was not enough. Although the steady drip of raindrops will pierce even stone, perhaps more water from another source was needed. Anyway, it was worth discussing with Oishi. Sometimes two minds were better than one.

It was early one morning in late summer when Fujii, the spy, arrived outside the house at Yamashina to take up his post.

He was yawning when he stopped before his basket-headed subordinate and asked for a report on the night's activities.

"Nothing," came the muffled answer. "No one in or out all night long."

Fujii frowned. This had been the pattern for several weeks now. And there had been very little movement discernible during the daytime. Was Oishi sick? Could he be worn out from all the partying in Kyoto? The lack of activity made Fujii suspicious and apprehensive. His reports to Chisaka nowadays sounded like Oishi had retired completely. But was this really the case? Or was it a trick, as he suspected the taking in of Okaru was a trick?

Thoughtfully, he dismissed his man and took up the guard post himself. It was hot inside the straw basket on his head and he knew it was going to get hotter before the day was over. If only something would happen to relieve the monotony.

Everything inside the house was apparently harmonious. On several occasions he had seen Oishi and Okaru come out for short walks in the garden and they had always seemed attentive to each other. Oishi's young son also seemed to have found a fitting companion in the little *maiko* and showed no signs of restlessness either. It was altogether too quiet from all standpoints. Something had to happen.

What did happen that morning was something he would never have been able to imagine. At a very early hour, Oishi came out of the house alone, carrying some unfamiliar implement. Fujii looked closer and saw that it was a hoe! And he was not only carrying it but looked like he was going to use it!

Fujii tipped back the basket on his head for a better look. Oishi was actually starting to prepare the soil in a little plot in front of the house. He was getting it ready for fall planting, of all things! Fujii was just getting used to this notion when Okaru came out the front entrance to watch. She had a few suggestions for Oishi as to just how to manage the hoe and what area to cover, and Fujii had to blink hard to make sure he was not dreaming. Was this the great warrior, the samurai he had been hired to follow to prevent a bloody uprising? He could never have imagined such a scene of domestic tranquility in connection with the ex-chief retainer of the house of Asano.

As the day grew warmer, Oishi stripped off his outer garment and went on working in his underclothes like any poor farmer. The heat affected Okaru, too, and she became more shrill in her comments and suggestions.

"That's not the way—you have to dig deeper than that!"

Oishi made no discernible reply, but kept on digging.

A little later, she spoke out again.

"Do you think that's a large enough area? We've got a lot of things to plant if we want our own fresh vegetables every day."

Oishi grunted and tried to keep digging but the perspiration was running into his eyes and he stopped to wipe it away with his hand.

"Don't stop now," she said loudly. "Let's finish up before it gets any hotter."

"I'd get through a lot sooner if you'd go in the house and shut your mouth," he shouted back at her.

She stood aghast for a moment at the way he had talked to her and then turned with a sob and ran into the house. Oishi cursed loudly to himself and set to work with a vengeance. And Fujii watched it all in amazement.

When he was relieved from his post, he quickly dashed off a letter to Chisaka informing him of these unexpected developments and because of it he was shortly thereafter summoned to Edo.

Chisaka stopped his pacing in front of Fujii as he caught the spy in a furtive yawn.

"Am I boring you?" he asked sarcastically.

"No, no," Fujii boomed out hastily. "It's just that we've been shorthanded and I haven't gotten much rest lately."

"If what you tell me is true," and here the oily little man stopped as he saw the tall samurai's hand fall lightly onto his sword. "What I mean is, if it is true that Oishi has indeed retired for good from active life, then you'll have plenty of chance to rest."

Fujii took a deep breath.

"I know the evidence points to his retirement as final, but I still have a feeling that all is not what it seems."

"I appreciate your sentiments. You've been on Oishi's trail for so long now, you probably don't want to give up. But *I* am the one who interprets the facts of your observations as you report them. And on the basis of the reports, I don't see how I can justify the expenditure of any more funds to Lord Uesugi."

Something in the way Chisaka said this made Fujii uneasy. He hoped he had not offended this little man who was in a position to do him good or harm.

"I am a soldier," he said simply. "I follow orders to the best of my ability and do not question my assignments. I accept your interpretation."

Chisaka smiled at this acknowledgment of his superiority, then cleared his throat and turned away.

"You have been a very valuable assistant, Fujii," he said finally. "And I intend to reward you for your services."

"All I ask is to be allowed to continue the privilege of serving the house of Uesugi," Fujii said with a humbleness he did not feel.

Chisaka turned to him and folded his arms. "That is something I wanted to talk to you about." He caught a glimpse of the thin man's eyes narrowing and hastily added, "Not that I don't want you for one of our bowmen—I know that you're an excellent archer—but there are other considerations. Financial, for one. You know how much this spying has cost our treasury in the past few months. And, as you know, the cost of supporting even one more fighting man has gone up tremendously, especially considering that we live in times of peace. I shouldn't tell you this, but we've had to reduce our forces lately and let men go that have been with the house of Uesugi all their lives. So you see it would look strange to bring you in."

Fujii could keep still no longer. "But don't you see that if you call off all spying and let Oishi come and go as he pleases, you will have only one last defense for Lord Kira, and that will be a large force of well-trained troops."

"I think we have a sufficient number of those," Chisaka said calmly.

"What is it you have against me to treat me like this?" Fujii burst out, standing to his full height as he spoke.

Chisaka was thoughtful for a moment.

"Why, only the fact that you remind me of the whole wretched Asano affair," he finally said matter-of-factly. "And I prefer to consider the matter closed."

Fujii closed his eyes. He had taken this dirty job because it promised him a chance to break away from the despised position of ronin. But now all that, along with his interview, was at a bitter end.

It was Okaru who first learned the good news. She had gone out of the house early to water the little plot of vegetables and sensed that something seemed out of place. She looked around, puzzled, uncertain for a moment what it was.

Then she looked out the gate toward the road and realized the truth. The spy was gone!

Quickly she hurried in to Oishi's bed and knelt beside him. He opened his eyes sleepily to look at her and then opened them wider as he saw her excited expression.

"What would you like more than anything else in the world?" she asked teasingly.

He smiled and reached out for her but she took his hand to help pull him to his feet. Then with a broad smile she led the mystified Oishi to the front entrance. He looked out and gasped.

For the first time since they had come to Yamashina there was no basket-headed *komuso* watching the house. Oishi flashed her a quick smile of gratitude, then let out a great shout that brought the others running and soon they were all chattering in excitement.

They soon discovered the cook was gone, too, and Oishi and Kataoka winked at each other as the others slowly realized that he had been another spy. Now there was real cause for celebration and Okaru and the little *maiko* took over in the kitchen to prepare a feast. The time of waiting was over and the men of Ako could move at last!

In Edo, Kira was not in a mood for celebrating. When the reports from the spies stopped coming, he went to call on Chisaka to find out what had happened. Chisaka, rubbing his bald head, told him simply that the expenses had become too great and the spying had been terminated.

"But what protection do we have..." began Kira, his frown lines deepening.

"Oh, don't worry so much," interrupted Chisaka with a forced laugh. "We've kept this up for months now—I think it's obvious they're not going to do anything."

"I'm not so sure," said Kira, shaking his head.

"The time for action would have been when the castle was confiscated—don't you agree? And since then they've made no move that could be called suspicious. Even when their leader came to Edo and you hid in your mansion, there was really nothing to worry about. He came to visit his master's grave, that's all."

"But I'd feel so much safer if..."

"Look, Lord Kira," Chisaka interrupted again, "I've arranged, with Lord Uesugi's permission, to assign guards to your house who will be instantly available in case of attack. This has meant extra work for me and extra expense for the house of Uesugi. Even though it seems unnecessary we are willing to continue this schedule indefinitely. But to ask for more..."

Kira suddenly understood two things. First, that if he wanted additional protection he would have to bribe Chisaka to furnish it. This he was unable to do from lack of funds now that his income had been reduced because of his retirement. He also saw that Chisaka was continuing to avoid the matter of taking him into the castle of Uesugi, and he felt the need to speak out.

"There was some discussion at one time about my moving into the castle..."

"No room," said Chisaka quickly, "and no necessity. You're just as safe where you are, believe me. We're close enough so that if there is trouble you can send for help, and I'll guarantee you reinforcements—although you're so capable a swordsman yourself, I don't see why you'd need them."

Kira was far from satisfied, but he saw there was nothing he could do but protest directly to the lord of the house and this he was reluctant to do because of the position occupied by his grandson. So he bade Chisaka good-bye and went home.

He would have been far more disturbed if he had known that Horibe had received a message from Hara telling him that the rumors about Oishi's behavior in Kyoto were true and that the time had come to take matters into their own hands. Horibe, in a flurry of excitement, immediately left for Osaka to confer secretly with his new leader. In view of the

circumstances they did not think there would be much difficulty in getting the majority of the men behind them.

It was at the archery school in Osaka later that same month
that the decision to launch an attack on Kira was made, but in
an unexpected manner.

Hara had called a night meeting of all the men in the area,
explaining that in view of Oishi's scurrilous behavior he was
no longer to be considered their leader. He announced that he
was taking over, with the help of Horibe, and they intended
to waste no time in planning and executing an attack on Kira's
mansion in Edo. Many declined to accept Hara's invitation,
still believing that their leader was capable, but a sizable number did turn out, and Hara was pleased to see that there were
enough to give them a chance.

In the dark gallery, lit only by a single torch, Hara had taken
the floor and was explaining why he felt justified in calling
such a meeting on his own, when there was a sudden knock
at the door.

Hara broke off and all the men held their breaths while the
guard at the door opened it a crack and looked out. They were
prepared to run or to fight, if necessary, but neither of these
measures proved necessary. They all saw the guard catch his
breath when he recognized the visitors and he closed the door
again in a highly flustered manner to hurry over to speak to
Hara.

"It's Oishi!" he whispered. "Oishi and Kataoka!"

Hara exchanged a quick glance with Horibe. There was a
moment of indecision, then Hara spoke.

"Let them in."

Horibe was about to protest but Hara's look silenced him.
After all, Oishi was still their official leader and they had no
alternative but to admit him if he requested it.

The guard hurried back to the door and opened it. Oishi, in a broad-brimmed peasant hat, entered with quiet dignity. He was followed by Kataoka, who was also dressed in the manner of a man of the fields. Oishi walked through the room, past the gay red-and-yellow archery targets that contrasted so strongly with the somber mood of those present, and finally came to a stop facing them all. He picked up a stray arrow from the floor and stripped the feathers from it as he spoke.

"I'm sorry to interrupt your gathering," he said calmly, as though he had walked in on nothing more than a tea party, "but a certain urgent matter has come up which will most likely affect your plans."

He looked around at them and some of the men moved uncomfortably, feeling that he might be memorizing their faces so he could take some reprisal against them later. Oishi sensed this and immediately tried to put their minds at rest.

"First let me say that I blame no one for being here tonight, nor do I bear any ill will toward those who assumed the authority to summon you."

Hara and Horibe looked at the floor and said nothing as Oishi continued.

"I am aware that many of you have lost faith in my ability to lead you because of things you've heard about my style of living in Kyoto. You've probably learned these things from Hara, who is an eyewitness to the fact that I have caroused with women of the lowest sort—and on money that of course belongs to you all."

Some of the men were beginning to shift around in embarrassment but Oishi kept on with his patient explanation.

"You may also have heard that I have been seen in public places in an intoxicated state and have even been caught brawling in a public theater...And I must tell you frankly that all these things are true."

Oishi ignored the low murmur that followed these words and laid down the arrow to turn directly to Hara.

"I had hoped, however, that my old friend Hara would have allowed me to explain my actions before jumping to unfounded conclusions and attempting to seize the leadership of our band for himself."

Hara made a gesture of protestation but Oishi continued.

"I appreciate his desire to do something about our master's death but I submit that it is no stronger than my desire to do the same. I also admire him for starting this school of archery for commoners, because I know from experience what depths we have had to sink to in order to prove to the world that we are what we are not. That was the point to all that I did and I am here to report to you that I have met with a measure of success."

He paused and looked at them with an air of satisfaction. "The spies have gone. For the first time since our master's death I feel it is now possible to go ahead with plans that have a chance of success. To have made a move before now would have been foolhardy, as I said all along."

There was a murmur among the men and Oishi turned to Hara.

"Where is your assistant—the one who calls himself Konishi?"

Hara hardly knew how to answer and stuttered in his reply.

"Why, he's—he's gone! I haven't seen him for two days!"

Oishi nodded. "You're lucky, Hara, that this meeting wasn't held two days ago. Isn't it obvious to you that your assistant was one of Fujii's men?"

Hara growled and was about to argue the point but Oishi went on without giving him a chance.

"Kataoka saw him here when he delivered my messages that you refused to receive. He recognized him as the man who was with you that night in Kyoto when you lost your faith in your leader... But let me ask you a question. How could you have found me that night unless the man who led you was in league with the spies? Did you ever stop to think about that?"

Hara's mouth fell open. There was no answer.

"Yes, the spies are gone," Oishi went on, "and I credit my acting ability for that accomplishment. I was so accomplished an actor I even fooled many of you, although you should have remembered that I took the same vows as you and have never stopped respecting them. Regardless of what has happened, however, I think we still have the same desire to avenge our master's death. We made promises to one another which I for one intend to keep. I hope you all feel the same."

There was a pause for a moment and then a general murmur of agreement swept through the room.

"Good," said Oishi, "because the time has finally come when we may speak of action not in terms of next year or next month, but of now! I received a message today from the acting head of the Edo group," and here he looked pointedly at the embarrassed Horibe who was far from his assigned post, "which tells us that as far as our petition is concerned, all is lost. Daigaku Asano has been placed in the custody of Asano-Akinokami in his province. He has been condemned to permanent exile for his brother's crime and the family name is to be excised from the official book of heraldry. All hopes for the recovery of the castle at Ako are dashed once and for all."

The men around him sat wide eyes as this terrible news sank into their minds. Then they began to mutter and the sound grew in subdued excitement.

"Revenge!" was the cry. "Now we can take our revenge at last," they said, and Hara walked falteringly to Oishi to bow before him.

"Is it true?" he asked. "Can we at last avenge Lord Asano's death as we should?"

Oishi nodded, his eyes flashing in the torch light.

"Once again," Hara said penitently, "I ask you to forgive me."

Oishi smiled and took his hand. Now Horibe came forward with apologies and Oishi included him in his smile of forgiveness. He beckoned to Kataoka and as the monkey-faced little man approached, Hara seized him in a bear hug of affection that brought an exaggerated gasp from his victim and a tension-breaking laugh from the crowd. Now they were all together again and nothing but death could divide them.

Chapter Sixteen

THERE WAS A FINALITY IN THE MESSAGE from Edo about Daigaku's banishment that brought both relief and despair to the house at Yamashina. It was obviously a bitter blow for Shindo and Koyama, who had pinned their hopes on winning out without a struggle. When Kataoka heard the news, his monkey face set in an expression of determination and the glint of battle came into his eyes. Chikara's first feeling was of having stepped off into space, but he kept one hand on his sword and pretended his feet were still on the ground.

After the first bitter moment, Oishi felt strangely at peace. For the first time since his master's death, the path of action was now clearly revealed. There would be no more arguments with his men about postponing what must be done. There would be no more playing the fool as he had so despised. There would be no more hiding his intentions, which were now to be fulfilled. They would kill the man responsible for Lord Asano's death, regardless of the consequences. The time for waiting was over.

At first there was fear that the news would bring back the spy force and Oishi was obliged to move cautiously, but after a few days went by and Fujii and his men did not appear, he sent out word for his men to assemble. It seemed evident now that Kira and his allies had taken the confiscation of the castle at Ako as final and had never considered that Daigaku had a chance with his appeal. The fact that Oishi had waited for the decision on the appeal now gave him an advantage he would never have had otherwise—that of surprise.

The men came to Yamashina in small groups in answer to Oishi's summons and within four days Horibe and the first small contingent of troops went up to Edo. The plan was for the rest to follow a few at a time so as not to create undue suspicion. Once in Edo, they were to use assumed names and stay apart until the last man, Oishi, arrived.

With Onodera, his old chief of staff, Oishi began to work out a schedule of departure. On paper their number had grown to about a hundred and twenty but it soon became apparent that this was a meaningless figure. More men than anticipated belonged to what Yoshida had called the "third group"—those who were with Oishi in his plan to get the castle restored, but who were suddenly unavailable when it came to embarking on the road to vengeance. For this reason he decided to send Kataoka among all the men to return their pledges and tell them that they were free to drop out. He knew some of them felt that they would be doing their aged parents or small children a disservice by abandoning them now and he wanted them to know there would be no prejudice against them if they decided not to go on. In the case of some of the followers, he took it on himself to reassure them personally.

One such that he visited was Emonshichi Yato, who was only seventeen, but who had already risked his life to tell Oishi about the meeting Hara had called in Osaka. The boy lived with his aged parents in Kyoto and Oishi went to call when he learned that Yato had reaffirmed his pledge. Since Chikara, who was also seventeen, was being allowed to go, he could not deny this boy on the grounds of age, but he wanted some assurance from his family that they approved.

It was plain from the crude hut they lived in that they were having a hard time of it, but they insisted that Yato be allowed to go. They told Oishi the boy would never live it down if he were refused permission to join the band and they would feel that they had let down their masters, meaning Lord Asano and Oishi himself.

Against this Oishi had no argument but more than ever he realized the dreadful responsibility he had taken on himself. It was up to him to see that the boy did not die in vain, as with all the others. He knew they would follow him wherever he would lead and in life or in death he would be haunted by their recriminations if he failed. As he was leaving the shack on the outskirts of the city, he was surprised to see one of the servants from the Ako castle bringing in a small supply of food to the old couple. The man behaved strangely, pretending not to recognize his old leader as he entered the shack, and Oishi was puzzled until a flash of insight told him what was happening. The servant was now actually supporting his former masters and did not want this to be known for fear of embarrassing them. Oishi shook his head in wonder, then moved away as a quiet sobbing came from the hut and a comforting voice responded, "It won't be so bad if you think of it as the time before we had a child."

Oishi also intended to visit Shindo and Koyama but he was thwarted in this by their sudden disappearance. It was much later when he finally received an apologetic note from Shindo saying that after due consideration he and Koyama had decided they were not cut out to be fighters and would only be a nuisance in battle. They had concluded that "of thirty-six devices it is best to take flight" and hoped he would forgive them. Oishi was not particularly surprised at their action and was glad they had been weeded out before it was too late. He commended their honesty in admitting their shortcomings, but he hoped too many others would not follow the same path.

The report from Kataoka that night was not encouraging. About half the men they had counted on had reneged, leaving less than sixty. Kataoka, too, had found much misery, including cases of children and old people being forced to work, and everywhere a profound sadness at the thought of the coming farewells. At any rate, they were sure of the men that were left—although that situation could change, too, when they assembled in Edo and their objective was clearly in view.

Seeing that Oishi was depressed by these developments Kataoka attempted to add a joking note by telling of one man who could not go because his wife would not let him—"She keeps him too well under her hips!"—but Oishi had already left the room.

He had not seen Okaru for several days because of the rush of activities that began with the message from Edo, but now when he wearily pushed open the door to his room he found her waiting for him. He was grateful for her presence and moved to lie down beside her. He was about to say something in apology for having neglected her, when she threw back the covers and flung her naked body onto him with a sob.

"Don't go," she pleaded. "Don't go to Edo with the rest of them—it's suicide!"

Surprised by her outburst, he took her arms from around his neck and held her hands together in front of him.

"You know better than that," he told her. "You, a trained geisha, so shamelessly displaying your feelings? What will your customer think?"

"I don't care," she wailed. "You're going up to Edo to die and I won't let you!"

"I think you must be a spy," he told her as he gently lay her down. "You know all my plans and you're trying to change them to benefit my enemy."

"I'm trying to change them to benefit myself," she sobbed as she turned away. "Think of my life. Think of saving it rather than of taking someone else's."

"Oh," he said as before. "Now you're threatening suicide. Is it fair to put me in a position like that? Besides, I know you would never do it."

"How do you know?" she sniffled.

"Because you're too strong," he told her, and rose on his elbow to look down at her. "You've fought your battle—you've regained your position—you're not the kind to stay defeated."

"But there's no recovery from some kinds of loss," she sniffed.

"You've got to give me the same chance you had," he said. "It's only fair."

"Nothing is fair," she answered bitterly. "And your killing one more scoundrel won't make it so. Have you no concern for your own life—or that of your family?"

Oishi paused for a moment. "One's life weighs lightly against duty," he told her at last.

"But duty to whom? Your master is dead—there's no one giving you orders now."

"Oh, but there is," he said in a faraway voice, and she lifted herself to look more closely into his face to try to guess his meaning. He placed his hand behind her head and kissed her as she lay back with a sigh. Then he started to make love to her in the gentle way she had taught him and after a while she responded, and much later they went to sleep.

It was the first week in October before Oishi was ready to leave. He had to obtain articles of arms and armor in Kyoto which he insisted on personally transporting because of the risk. When these were ready, the last of the men had already gone ahead except for Onodera, Kataoka, Chikara, and three others, including the servant Mimura who had a special mission to perform.

It was early one cool autumn morning when they assembled in front of the house and loaded the remaining horses with the crates of "silk goods" they were transporting. All the men were disguised as ordinary porters who would walk the long Tokaido with wares consigned to a wealthy daimyo in Edo.

In the manner of a geisha-house farewell, Okaru and the little *maiko,* both in their gayest kimono, came to the front of the house to see them off. They laughed as though it was the end of a weekend of pleasure with many more to look forward to. Young Chikara bowed a polite farewell to Okaru who smiled mistily; she would never forget that she owed her life to him. Then he turned to the little girl and bowed to her, too. At this, she could no longer hold back her tears and turned quickly to hide her face in Okaru's sleeve. Chikara turned away and took his place in the caravan. Oishi raised his arm to give the command to move out, then hesitated.

"You know..." he said to Okaru, but he could not go on. His arm came down and the men slowly moved out with their horses. Okaru smiled bravely to the last, but when they were out of sight beyond the gate the smile faded and her pretty red fan fell from her hand. The autumn wind had already begun to blow. She took the little *maiko* by the hand and led her in to prepare for her return to Gion alone. Okaru's own chance to go back had been forfeited by her refusal to spy on Oishi, for that was the price Hoshino had been willing to pay.

Chapter Seventeen

MIMURA LEFT SEVERAL HOURS ahead of the others. He had been entrusted with a mission of the utmost importance and his chest swelled as he thought of the responsibility that had been entrusted to him.

He, too, was dressed as an ordinary porter, but his route did not lie directly in the direction of Edo. Instead he took the road to Kyoto, a dim path to follow in the predawn darkness. He entered the city and made directly for the district where the Emperor held his court. At a certain back gate on a side street he stopped, looked around to see that he was not observed, and knocked lightly.

No light went on inside, but in a moment he heard someone coming and the gate slowly opened. He heard a flurry of movement from inside and what sounded like a woman's muffled sob before a small form stepped out alone. It was Lord Asano's little daughter, dressed as a commoner, but with a bright, eager expression on her aristocratic little face that gave her away as anything but a peasant.

Without a word to those inside, Mimura took her by the hand and started to walk rapidly away. Oishi had already thanked the foster parents in the letter which had set up this meeting and the clumsy servant had no wish to waste time now when every moment was precious.

The sun was beginning to break over the rooftops of Yamashina when he arrived back at the junction of the road that led to Edo. His arrival had been timed perfectly. Along the road from Yamashina at that very moment came Oishi and the rest of the group, walking beside their pack horses.

They could not help expressing their joy at seeing the child and welcomed her in low voices. She ran to Oishi and threw herself in his arms and after a brief, silent embrace he picked her up and put her on the back of one of the horses. He motioned to Mimura to take the bridle of this horse and to drop back behind the main body of men. There was always the danger that they might be recognized and he wanted Lord Asano's daughter to appear to be traveling separately. Mimura would always be within shouting distance in case of an emergency.

They were in no hurry. Oishi still believed the roundabout way was best and purposely took his time. At night they often camped by the side of the road rather than risk being seen in an inn where sharp eyes and wagging tongues could do them damage. At a slow walking pace, it took them ten days to reach the Hakone Pass.

The trip so far was uneventful with not a single spy in evidence. For this reason, and because his future now seemed so clear-cut, Oishi was able to relax and enjoy the scenery he had been too preoccupied to notice before. Now he could appreciate the spectacular sights of the countryside in the fall and majesty of Mt. Fuji as never before.

There was a barrier at Hakone, the last one before descending to the Kanto Plain, but they had successfully passed all others and Oishi was confident they could convince the gatekeepers that they were on legitimate business.

Still, he approached it at night, just to be on the safe side. There was a cold wind blowing, which gave them an excuse to turn up the collars of their long cloaks and also guaranteed that the guards would not stay long outside their warm huts.

It went as Oishi had planned. The guards were in a hurry to get back inside and did not even inspect their goods. It was over quickly and again they were on their way, Oishi in the lead. It seemed as though nothing could stop them now.

As they started the long descent, however, a lone horseman appeared on the road approaching them. Oishi wrapped his cloak tighter and turned aside as the man passed but then he drew in his breath sharply as he recognized who it was. The tall, thin figure of the man who had been following him for so long was unmistakable. It was the ronin Fujii!

There was nothing he could do to warn the others and his hand went to his sword beneath his cloak. The man on horseback looked over every man in the group carefully and it seemed impossible that he should not know them. Yet he rode on silently without a sign of recognition. Oishi watched him till he disappeared from view, then motioned to the others to halt. For their own safety it would be best to put on all speed, but his first thought was of the little girl. Until she came safely in view, they would wait.

As he left Oishi's group behind and his horse climbed toward the guard station, Fujii's head was spinning. He had dared not challenge Oishi at first sight because he was outnumbered and would have been cut down in a second. But what would Chisaka give to know that his worst fears had been realized and the men of Ako were on the march? He had only to notify the guards at the barrier and Oishi would be held for the Shogun's disposal. He would surely be rewarded—perhaps even given a permanent position with Uesugi's troops.

That had been his first inclination. But now, as he came closer to the guard shack, he began to have second thoughts. Was anyone paying him for spying now? Did he have any responsibility toward a former employer who had failed to live up to his promises? And what if there were a reward—would it be enough to pay for what he might lose?

He reached the guard shack and stopped. The men came out into the cold grumbling and asked him the routine questions about his identity and destination. It was easier to leave Edo than to get into it. He was tempted to share his secret with them, just to see the shocked look on their faces, but the word loyalty kept coming to his mind and he kept silent. When he had satisfied them, they went back inside and he turned once to look in the direction from whence he had come, then kicked his horse into a walk. His first loyalty was to his reputation as a samurai, even an ex-samurai, and he knew that his own honor was at stake. What business of his was it if a fellow samurai entered Edo? Especially someone like Oishi, whom he had come to respect, now more than ever?

As he moved along the path, he saw a ragged fellow approaching with a child on a horse. He could not identify the man because he was walking on the opposite side of his horse, although his ungainly walk was vaguely familiar. The child meant nothing to him. It only crossed his mind that it was a cold night and such young ones should be home in bed. He shivered a little, wrapped his cloak tighter about him, and went on with a curiously peaceful smile.

At Kamakura, thirty miles from Edo, Oishi and his group stopped. They rested here for three days, still apprehensive about the encounter with Fujii, but when no troops appeared to take them into custody they began to breathe more easily. At the great bronze statue of Buddha, Oishi gave thanks for their safe journey, as did the other members of his party. Now Oishi sent Chikara ahead as a scout and the rest of them moved to Kawasaki, closer still to Edo.

While they waited impatiently for some word that it was safe to go ahead, they passed the time watching the fish in the stream beside which they had made their camp. Here, for the first time since leaving Yamashina, Oishi felt secure enough to approach the little girl.

"How did you like your life in the Emperor's world?" he asked as he sat beside her on a rock by the sparkling water.

"Oh, it was wonderful, uncle," she said. "The family was so nice to me—they treated me like their own daughter. I had music lessons and calligraphy right along with their own children. And we had parties, too, and celebrated all the festivals."

Oishi nodded. He had hoped it would be like that.

"You know, don't you, that life with your mother may be a great deal different? She may be confined to her parents' home for a long time to come and you will be expected to share her exile."

She nodded. "I know."

"But you still want to go to your mother, don't you?"

"Oh, yes," she said without hesitation. "That's my proper place, as everyone knows."

Oishi smiled. Getting her back to her mother had been almost as important in his mind as getting the house restored, and now such an accomplishment was within his grasp.

They were still sitting together talking about her experiences in Kyoto when Chikara appeared on the bank waving to them, and they hurried to see what he had to say.

"It's safe to go ahead," he reported, and Oishi wasted no time in summoning the others and packing to leave.

They split up and entered the city separately. Now Oishi accompanied the girl while the rest went to establish headquarters at a central inn. First they would dispose of the goods they were carrying at a "fencing school" which Horibe had recently established. It was an appropriate place to store the arms they had smuggled in from Kyoto.

Oishi kept his promise to himself not to see Lady Asano again, although it required a tremendous effort on his part not to go with the little girl to her meeting with her mother. He had sent no advance notice of his intentions, but relied on his memory of the layout of her parents' garden to know how to find the back gate and let her in. The joyous cries he heard over the wall were all the reward he needed for a job well done and he smiled as he heard them.

Then he reluctantly turned away and went to join his men.

"I don't like it," Hara muttered. He had come to the inn in Nihombashi where Oishi was staying with Onodera and Chikara to report on the situation as it existed.

"There are over sixty of us in Edo now," he went on, shaking his head, "certainly enough to raise some attention somewhere. How can it be that neither Kira nor the Shogun is aware of our presence?"

"It does seem strange," Oishi agreed, "that we seem to be so invisible."

"I'm afraid they're laying for us. As soon as we make a move they'll be all over us by the hundreds."

Oishi nodded. This was what he had been thinking, too.

"There are only two possibilities," he told Hara. "Either they actually don't know we're here or they're waiting, as you say, for us to start something. I'm inclined to believe the latter is the case. After all, what laws are we breaking by coming to Edo? None. Therefore no one has any legal grounds for challenging us."

"But I don't think we're even being watched!" Hara interjected.

"Possibly not. They don't need to watch us—they only have to watch Kira. That's much simpler and requires fewer men."

"In that case, shouldn't we attack quickly before their guard can become too well organized?"

"That's a good point," Oishi was forced to agree, "but it's even more important that our strike, when it comes, has the advantage of such careful planning that failure will be impossible."

Hara mumbled to himself, then nodded.

"You're right—you're right, as always."

"The first thing I want to do," Oishi said, "is to get a look at the situation for myself. Will you meet me in the morning and take me to Kira's?"

Hara's eyes flashed. "Nothing would give me more pleasure—except to see Kira's head rolling in the dirt."

"At dawn then, we'll meet by the bridge across the Sumida—the one nearest here that crosses into Honjo. We'll be disguised as servants on our way to work."

The next morning Oishi was strangely excited. He felt as though he had come to the end of a long road with everything he wanted waiting at the other end. For the first time he was going to see his master's enemy!

He met Hara as scheduled and they crossed into the ward of Honjo, then entered Matsuzaka where Kira's mansion was. They met few passers-by in the streets at this early hour, but there were a great many dogs and Oishi began to fear that they would be a problem during the attack. A body of armed men might disturb them and set off an alarm of howling that could alert their enemies. He would have to think of something to do about that.

Now they approached the front of Kira's gate and slowed to inspect it as they passed. It was well built and too heavy for them to think of battering down. They also noted slits high up where archers could fire down on them and peepholes below where all who entered had to show their faces.

They leisurely circled the entire estate and found a rear gate that was no less formidable than the one in front. Horibe had of course reported on all these features in detail and had even obtained a floor plan of the house, but Oishi still wanted to see them himself before he drew up final plans for the attack.

When they arrived back at the front gate, they took up positions at an open market across the road and waited. They were there for much of the morning and began to fear they would be questioned by the proprietor when they heard the gate start to open.

A squad of archers ran out and formed in ranks. Then an ornate palanquin was quickly carried out, followed by another squad of archers, and the whole procession moved away down the street. Oishi had to look fast, but he was rewarded at last. Inside the palanquin was the unmistakable figure of Kira, recognizable from all the descriptions he had heard. It was only a brief glimpse, but he would never forget that scowling face and blackened teeth. This was the face he swore he would next see before him at the end of a long sword.

He turned to Hara and realized that he had been holding his breath. He let it out long and slowly.

"I think that's all we need to see for now," he said, and they returned quietly to where the others were waiting.

Chapter Eighteen

OISHI'S MEN WERE NOW SCATTERED all over Edo. So far they seemed to have escaped detection by the local authorities, but they paid for their secrecy in terms of not being a single unified force.

Hara and Horibe acted as deputy commanders and relayed Oishi's messages to subordinate group leaders who in turn passed the word along to each individual samurai. Since they still had no idea when or where the decisive attack would be made, Oishi's first order was for each man to become familiar with the area around Kira's mansion and, if possible, to learn to know Kira by sight. He had to trust that none of them would become too aroused at the sight of the black-toothed scoundrel and make a single-handed attempt on his life. In his message he stressed the fact that Kira's guards were well trained, and that any rash act against their master would be easily put down. Furthermore, such a move would alert all of Edo to their presence and their chance of eventual success would be doomed.

So far it was working out as he had planned. The men, alone or in small groups, received their introduction to Kira by casually passing by his gate at times when it was calculated he would be coming or going. Their tours of duty were of varying lengths and no one stayed long. The only exception was a permanent guard stationed over a shop directly across from the mansion. He kept a complete log on all arrivals and departures, and Kira's palanquin was discreetly followed to learn the pattern of their enemy's affairs. The question was, how long could they keep this up before Kira's guards began to recognize them?

Yoshida recognized another very real danger as well.

"We're extremely vulnerable in one way, Oishi-dono," he said one night at a strategy meeting with Hara, Horibe, and Onodera in Oishi's room at the inn.

"What's that?" Oishi asked in concern.

"We're all completely dependent on you for our directions... Not that I would have it any other way," he added hastily as Oishi's brow furrowed. "But wouldn't it be more reasonable for you to guard your person more carefully?"

Oishi shook his head at the prospect of limiting his own movements, but the others agreed with Yoshida.

"There are 'accidents' that could happen to you if Kira willed it," Hara said.

"But I can't travel around with an armed guard," Oishi snapped. "What good would I be to anyone?"

"Perhaps the answer is not to travel at all," Yoshida suggested. "A squad of four or five fighting men could stay here with you at all times."

"I think he's right, Oishi-dono," Horibe put in. "You're taller and more easily recognized than the rest of us. As time goes by, you'll be spotted as a spy, if not actually identified as Lord Asano's chief retainer."

Oishi fretted for a moment and then sighed.

"I hate to think of shutting myself off—I had so much of that for so long in Yamashina."

"I sympathize with you," Hara said, "but what can you gain by seeing your enemy again?"

"Nothing, I suppose...I had hoped to be able to see Daigaku, but his confinement is well enforced. Still, perhaps it's just as well. I don't want him involved in our plans if I can help it."

The others nodded. This was the best way.

"Have all the men had a chance to see Kira by now?" Oishi asked abruptly.

Hara hesitated and looked at Horibe. He cleared his throat and prepared to speak, his eyes strangely downcast, when they were interrupted by a quiet knock at the door. Horibe opened it a crack, then quickly let in a grinning Kataoka.

The monkey-faced man bowed courteously to Oishi, nodded to the others and found a place to sit on the floor.

"You look pleased with yourself," Oishi observed.

Kataoka's grin grew broader.

"I've discovered a new diversion for rich merchants like myself in Edo."

"Oh? And what do the visiting merchants find to occupy themselves with in Edo nowadays?"

"Lessons," Kataoka said in confidential tones. "Lessons in the tea ceremony."

"Tea ceremony!" Oishi exploded.

The others looked at one another in surprise. Had Kataoka lost his mind to be playing games with them at a time like this?

"Of course I know the ceremony better than he does," Kataoka went on calmly, "but the tea master talks a lot and that part is entertaining."

"I'm glad you're amused," Oishi said sarcastically. "Some of us are not so fortunate in being able to choose the way we spend our time."

But Kataoka was not the kind to take a gentle hint.

"I learn much gossip of the court from my teacher," he went on imperturbably. "About many of those in high places."

"And how does this help us?" Hara asked impatiently. "I couldn't care less about the gossip of the court."

"But it would be nice to know Kira's plans in advance, wouldn't it?"

"Of course it would."

"Well, my teacher has a client who should be an excellent source for such information."

"And who is this client?" Hara asked wearily.

"I thought you'd never ask. He used to be court Master of Ceremonies. His name is Kira."

All those present reacted in pleased surprise. Kataoka had indeed made progress.

"Well done, Kataoka," Oishi said with a smile. "I knew you weren't just wasting our time."

"I didn't," Hara growled, and then laughed along with the rest of them.

Onodera nodded his gray head.

"I can't think of a better way to keep up with Kira's social life—and as it appears, that's what we need to know about most. If we can pin him down to a specific place and time..."

There was no need to say more. All were busy with their own thoughts until Oishi remembered some unfinished business.

"Hara, you were reporting on the men's tours of duty. Did you say that there are still some who haven't seen Kira?"

Again Hara hesitated.

"That is true."

"And for what reason?"

Hara scowled at the floor. This was the kind of report he hated to make.

"Because some of the men on the list have—disappeared."

"Disappeared," Oishi echoed bitterly. "You mean deserted, don't you?"

Hara made no answer and Oishi sighed.

"How many have left us?"

"About a third of our force."

"And you didn't mention this before?" Oishi asked in some anger.

"It makes no difference," Hara said doggedly. "We'll go ahead without them."

"You shouldn't be too surprised," Onodera said gently to Oishi. "You yourself said some men would turn from us when the scent of battle was actually in the air."

Oishi nodded.

"I know. Forgive my outburst." He shot a glance at Horibe. "You were right, Horibe, when you said time was against us. How could I expect to keep the men at a fever pitch for battle when I kept putting them off?"

Horibe shook his head.

"It's not time that's working against us—only fear."

"Caused partly by the disunity of our organization," Oishi said, "which will become worse with my isolation."

He sighed. A drastic move was evidently called for. In spite of the dangers involved, it was important to do something about their unity. He went to the door and beckoned to the man outside.

"Mimura," he said as the servant stepped in, "I have a special mission for you."

Mimura's head bobbed rapidly as he listened.

"I want you to find a suitable place—a public restaurant, perhaps—where we can all assemble."

"All of us?" asked Hara in alarm.

"Yes," Oishi said grimly. "It's time for one last meeting to reaffirm our purposes before our 'fighting men' drift away, one by one."

The others murmured among themselves in concern but Oishi continued with his instructions to the servant. It was essential that the loyal band grow no smaller.

After a few days of searching, Mimura found that Oishi's suggestion of a public restaurant as a meeting place was a good one. They could meet in the middle of the day like any other group of merchants and call themselves a "social group."

In Fukagawa, a central district of the city, he found an inn with large private dining rooms and reserved one on the ground floor. His reasoning was that in a downstairs room they would have a better chance of fighting their way out of any trap that might be sprung. He asked to see the kitchen on the pretext that his group was particular about the food it was served, and noted the location of the rear door for use in case of an emergency. He also asked that his party be disturbed as little as possible during the meal as the financial measures under discussion would require great concentration.

When the arrangements were completed, Oishi sent out word to all the Ako men remaining in Edo and on the appointed day they began to gather. Mimura entered the dining room with Oishi, then went to make one last inspection of the kitchen to be sure the rear exit was unobstructed. He had barely put his head in the door, however, before he quickly closed it and ran white-faced back to Oishi.

"We can't meet here," he spluttered excitedly.

"Tell me what's wrong, Mimura," said Oishi gruffly. "I'll decide whether we meet here or not."

"I'm sorry," Mimura apologized. "I'm sorry if I overstepped my bounds..."

"Get to the point," Oishi said. "What is the matter?"

"It's the boy—the fire boy who was in our house in Edo before...before our Lord Asano's death. He's here in this kitchen! Fortunately, I got out before he saw me. But if he should come into the dining room for any reason..."

Oishi thought rapidly. "The chances are if he's only a kitchen helper, he won't be serving us... How did you happen to miss him before? I thought you'd inspected this place and found it safe?"

"I'm sorry," Mimura said in abject apology. "He wasn't here the other day. I should have checked this morning...it is an oversight I most seriously regret."

"There's no help for it now," said Hara, who had entered in time to learn of their difficulty. "We must move elsewhere."

"We can't switch our plans at this late date," objected Oishi. "Everyone will be here soon. We have no alternative but to go ahead and meet as planned."

"But if the boy sees any of us from the old house..." said Mimura despairingly.

"If he does," interrupted Oishi, "it will be your job to take care of him. You got us into this, you'll have to get us out... Sit by the door leading to the kitchen. Listen for approaching servants and warn us when they're coming. You can clear your throat or propose a toast or something. And if the servant who enters is that wretched fire boy, I want you to cause him to die a "natural death" on the spot. How to do it I leave up to you. Understood?"

Mimura nodded helplessly.

"Now take your place. The meeting will be starting any minute and we don't want to cause any delays."

With a quick look around, Oishi went to take his place at the head of the table. Mimura stationed himself as ordered and Kataoka sat beside him to furnish aid if required. The others were now beginning to arrive.

When they were all present, the lunch began and Oishi was relieved to see that the serving was all handled by waitresses. The dishes were brought rapidly and the girls then withdrew in accordance with their instructions. Now Oishi called for everyone's attention. He wasted no time in getting to the point.

"Comrades," he began, with great emotion in his voice, "I'm glad to see you all here. The time we've been waiting for is near, and final plans must be made. Before going ahead, I must know who I can count on. With fewer men than this we cannot hope to succeed. I hope you can appreciate that fact and will respond honestly."

There was a murmur of agreement and he continued, much encouraged. He announced that he had a new oath to present which they were all to sign in blood. He paused and then began to read it to them.

"No matter what one's assignment may be in this matter, or no matter how menial one might consider such an assignment, there shall be no difference in honor or merit between one follower and the next, provided that he fulfills his duty to the best of his ability. Each of us must help the others at all times, seeking no individual glory. It must also be thoroughly understood..."

He was suddenly interrupted by Mimura who was coughing loudly. "A toast," he called out, "a toast to Hara, I mean Harano, the rice dealer!"

"To Harano, the rice dealer," the others echoed and drank down their cups of saké as a waitress entered from the kitchen to check their progress.

"To the drapery dealer from Kyoto," called out Mimura next and the others repeated the toast and drank to Kataoka, who grinned sheepishly. Then the waitress was gone and Oishi concluded reading the pledge.

"It must be thoroughly understood that none of us are free to act as we wish even after Kira has been killed. Procedures to be followed then will depend on circumstances we cannot foresee and will be announced at that time."

The men murmured in approval and when lunch was over and they came to bid farewell to their leader each signed his name in blood. There were forty-seven signers to this document, including one man in his seventies; five in their sixties, including Yoshida and Onodera; four in their fifties, including Hara; four in their forties, including Oishi; eighteen in their thirties, including Kataoka and Horibe; thirteen in their twenties, including Onodera's son Koemon; and Yato and Chikara, who were both seventeen. Each was handed detailed instructions as to armor, weapons, signals, meeting places, and names of their immediate leaders. The actual time and place of the attack remained to be set. All else was decided.

The men went as they had come, in twos and threes, until only Oishi and Mimura were left. Oishi now permitted himself to relax and even smile. Mimura came toward him tentatively with a crooked little smile of his own and they went out together, both pleased at the success of the meeting.

After a moment some kitchen helpers came in to clear the tables. One of them was the fire boy from Lord Asano's mansion. He was picking up some dishes at Oishi's place when he noticed a soiled napkin on the floor. He picked it up and looked at it curiously. It was covered with dots of blood and he threw it onto the table distastefully. If his curiosity had been more intense, he might have counted the stains and found that there were exactly forty-seven.

Not to be outdone by Kataoka, Hara established his own contact with Kira's household. He opened a rice shop and actually got their enemy's kitchen steward for a customer. The steward demanded a large discount so that Hara actually sold the rice for less than he paid for it, but in this case a business loss could be profitable in other ways. He was not allowed to deliver the rice inside Kira's gates—the security measures were much too strict for that—but he was in a position to know when extra quantities of rice might be needed for entertainment purposes. Horibe had already befriended a priest who was a social acquaintance of Kira's; some of the other followers used their own methods to try to pin down the movements of their elusive quarry.

But it was Kataoka, through his tea master, who got the first real lead.

He had gone for his weekly lesson and was bravely sipping the poorly made tea from an oversized cup when the tea master was called to the door to receive a message. While his back was turned, Kataoka dumped the tea into the *hibachi,* but the tea master, a cherubic fellow with a shaved head like a priest, was so excited when he returned that he failed to notice.

"Guess what," he gushed. "I've been invited to a party!"

"That's nice," murmured Kataoka, as he pretended to sip from his cup. "It must be an important occasion to give you so much pleasure."

"Oh, it is! At Lord Kira's house..."

Kataoka caught his breath and held it.

"...a ceremonial tea on the morning of December 6. I'm so *flattered* that he's asked me. I haven't been in Edo long, but already I'm beginning to make my way in society."

"Yes," said Kataoka, "you certainly are. And the ceremonial is to be at Lord Kira's house?"

"Yes, at his mansion. Oh, I wish I could take you with me. You've never been inside a real Edo mansion, have you?"

"No," lied Kataoka, who was remembering back to that fateful morning when Lord Asano had gone out of his mansion for the last time.

"But of course I haven't the right to invite you. I understand Lord Kira is very particular about his guests and has guards to check the invitations. Do you suppose he's still afraid some of Lord Asano's followers might be after him?"

"I don't know why he should think that—after so long a time."

"Yes—that's the way I look at it. If they really wanted revenge, they would have taken it a long time ago."

Kataoka nodded as the man talked on.

"It only goes to show that the day of the samurai is over, after all. When they don't uphold their own code, what can they expect will happen to the morals of the rest of the country?"

Kataoka gritted his teeth and said nothing.

"Anyway, it promises to be a grand occasion at Lord Kira's. Now then, shall we get back to our lesson?"

Kataoka obediently raised the empty cup to his lips and pretended to sip, turning it a little at a time as etiquette required. The morning of the sixth, he was thinking, meant that an attack could be mounted on the evening of the fifth with reasonable assurance that their man would be at home.

Kataoka had already reported the party to Oishi when word came from other sources that it had been postponed. The monkey-faced man scheduled an extra session with his tea master and learned that this was indeed true. The tea master was tearfully disappointed and could only hope that another chance would come. It seemed that the Shogun was having a party on the same date and Kira had canceled his own arrangements so that he could attend.

The men's spirits were deflated, but the following week when Kataoka went for his lesson they were again given reason for hope. This time he learned that there would definitely be a year's end party at Kira's some time in December. He relayed this to Oishi and the report was confirmed by Horibe, whose priest friend had asked him to deliver a letter of acceptance to the same party to Kira's gate.

The party was set for the fourteenth and Oishi felt a cold chill when he heard the date. Kataoka and Horibe recognized its significance, too, and gave Oishi meaningful glances. It was the same day of the month as Lord Asano's death and a sure omen that the time to strike had come at last!

Chapter Nineteen

SNOW BEGAN TO FALL ON THE NIGHT of the eleventh. It was a heavy fall and looked as if it would continue for several days. The people in the streets were heavily wrapped, hurrying, and had no eye for such things as the movements of strangers. It was ideal weather for the conspirators from Ako.

Oishi's final plan was simple: a simultaneous attack on both Kira's front and rear gates with his full force. Once the gates were taken, the older men would stay by them to guard against outside interference while the younger ones would enter the house to find their man.

Oishi would lead the assault on the front gate and the subsequent invasion of the house itself; Hara would be in charge at the rear and Onodera and Yoshida would command the forces outside. Weapons and uniforms had all been obtained and would be donned just before the attack. Every man knew his place and his target; now there was nothing to do but wait.

As the morning of the twelfth came and then the thirteenth the snow still fell, but there was no word of cancelation or postponement of Kira's party. The excitement of the men from Ako grew day by day and Oishi felt as exhilarated as any of them.

On the morning of the fourteenth, he went alone to Sengaku-ji temple to pay his last respects to Lord Asano. It was the first time he had risked being free of the surveillance of his guards and he knew he was taking a risk, but it was less conspicuous to go by himself than with a small army.

In the cemetery he wiped the snow from the plaque before Lord Asano's grave and once again raised his head to speak with his dead master.

"We are ready, my Lord, to take revenge."

He paused and imagined that these words brought the same satisfaction to Lord Asano's ears as they did to his own.

"Your loyal forces have gathered. Before the night is over some or all of us may have sacrificed our lives, but we count it as nothing because our cause is duty and our cause is honorable.

"Whether we succeed or not, we are sure to join you soon and this gives us courage in our undertaking. The forces we oppose are superior in number but with our spirit we are sure to vanquish them—or to die trying. We will have the element of surprise on our side and with luck will be able to find our man quickly with no unnecessary shedding of blood."

Once again he pledged his loyalty to the death and then with a deep bow of respect, he left Sengaku-ji.

At the corner where the pathway to the cemetery joined the post road stood a small country inn and as Oishi passed he could hear music and drunken shouting. He frowned at the image this brought to his mind of samurai misbehaving; this was indeed typical of Edo.

But then his brow unwrinkled as the clear notes of a samisen were heard and a girl began to sing. He smiled and then felt a twinge of remorse. He saw Okaru's face before him and knew that the days with her at Yamashina would haunt him as long as he lived. He sighed and after a while he moved thoughtfully away.

At the gateway to the inn, almost hidden by the snow, a blind beggar called for alms. Oishi almost stumbled over him, then walked on. After a few steps, however, he stopped. The beggar had a sword beside him, a samurai sword, and Oishi could not ignore it. For all he knew it could bear the crest of Asano—it could be one of his own men who had struck bottom.

He went back to the beggar, gave him a few coins, and started to walk away again. Then for the second time he stopped. This time when he returned to face the sightless eyes of the man in the snow he turned his coin purse upside down in his basket. Now as he stepped off into the snowy street he felt a sense of release, of peace and freedom. Money was something he need not worry about any more.

"It was to remind me how lucky we are that the beggar was placed in my path," he told Chikara, as they huddled close to the *hibachi* in the freezing little room at the inn.

"You see," he went on, "some people live all their lives without knowing which path is right. They're buffeted by this wind or that and never really know where they're going. That's largely the fate of the commoners—those who have no choice over their destiny. For those of us born as samurai, life is something else. We know the path of duty and we follow it without question."

He got up to look out the window as he continued.

"But even that may not be easy because there may be insurmountable obstacles. Such as what that blind beggar faces. He might have a secret dream of revenge against an oppressor, too. He might have justice on his side as we do now, but there is nothing he can do about it. I say we're lucky—we know what has to be done and it's within our capability to make it happen!"

Chikara's eyes were shining as his father spoke and he was about to make some reply when Oishi suddenly started and leaned forward to peer out the window more closely.

Two horsemen were approaching through the snow, one large and one small, and for a moment Oishi saw himself and Lord Asano's little daughter, riding through the fields of Ako on that day so long ago.

"Father..." Chikara said tentatively, and Oishi turned to look at him. For a moment he forgot what he had been saying, then he picked up where he had left off, but in a more subdued manner.

"As I was saying, we are lucky, lucky."

"I know we are, Father."

Oishi smiled at him. "That's right. Those are the words of a samurai. Remember, there's sacrifice involved in any kind of life. Even the man who chooses the safe way has to give up the thrill of combat. The point is that once you know what you want, you must be prepared to sacrifice everything to get it. Those who realize this are the fortunate ones. Those who know and can try. What more can a man ask for than that?"

Chikara shook his head. To him, too, there was nothing more important, and his father was reassured by his manner that it had not been a mistake to allow him to join the band.

Still, there were memories...

At the evening meal, which they ate together, Oishi was suddenly reminded of the boy's mother and his mind went from there to picture all the little ones around the table—the little ones that he had sent away. He was overcome by emotion for a moment, but hid his feelings from his son.

"Go easy on the rice," he told the boy, clearing his throat. "You'll be better off later without too much food in you."

Chikara nodded and obeyed, although he was still hungry. There was no meat or fish, of course, and other delicacies were ruled out for spiritual reasons. It would be bad luck to indulge oneself before going into such a solemn undertaking as faced them now.

After dinner they lay down for a short rest, although neither of them could sleep. Chikara reviewed his own part in the attack in his mind and then fell to thoughts of the past. He pictured his mother and little brother and sister and then the young *maiko* he had known so briefly. There was not the slightest chance he would ever see her again, but still he could not help thinking about her...

They were "awakened" promptly at eight by the arrival of Kataoka and Onodera, who spoke in whispers which seemed to emphasize the solemnity of the occasion. In silence they rose and dressed and went out into the snow.

The first meeting place for Oishi's group was Horibe's fencing school, where they changed into battle dress. There were three such places designated, with all the men to join together when they were ready to march.

Their clothes were new, both as a symbol of purity to ensure divine protection and as evidence that they were not driven to their extreme action by the desperation of poverty. Over wadded silk undergarments they put on cloth shirts that fastened close to the wrist. Next came a bloomerlike skirt that afforded great flexibility of movement. Over these came a coat of mail covered with satin and on top of this each man wore a lacquer-scaled breastplate with cross-stitching of silk cord and a great gold crest. A mantle and hood of broadcloth which could easily be tossed off gave them the appearance of officers of the fire brigade, a disguise they hoped would permit them to go unchallenged on their march through the streets.

Oishi had secretly had these outfits made at various armorers in Kyoto, a few at a time so as not to excite undue suspicion. When they were dressed, they moved out in twos and threes to Hara's rice shop, the final rendezvous point.

Here Oishi inspected each man and questioned all about their orders. He had finished this task and was sitting quietly, waiting for the hour to march, when he was startled to have a cup of saké handed to him. He turned to see the grizzled face of Hara.

It was time to propose one last toast to their success and this he did in a confident manner that inspired them all. Then it was time to leave.

Outside they formed in ranks of four and stepped off on Oishi's command. They carried two light ladders and appeared to be nothing more than a fire brigade on patrol, a not uncommon sight in the tinderbox alleys of Edo. The only difference was that at the rear of the column Mimura carried a placard with a statement of their intentions which would be displayed at the proper time.

The snowfall had stopped, but enough snow lay underfoot to deaden the sound of their footsteps. No one appeared on the streets except an occasional fire watcher who beat his sticks together to show that he was on the alert. Oishi returned their salutes and they were not challenged.

They had crossed the bridge over the Sumida River into Honjo and were entering Matsuzaka when the first incident occurred. A dog, mangy and shivering, stood in their path and began to growl as they approached. Fearful that the dog would bark and cause an alarm, Oishi gave a silent signal to Hara beside him. Without breaking his step, Hara put an arrow to his bow and let the animal have it full in the throat. With a gargle the dog fell dead and the men marched on past. As they looked at its corpse, they all realized that this was the first overt act of disobedience to the Shogun's law that had been committed since the band was formed. In itself, it made them liable for severe punishment, and they knew this was only the beginning.

To Hara's lips, the sight of the dog brought a chuckle. He was pleased at his marksmanship besides being keenly aware that they had passed the point of no return on their way to the final battlefield. This was what he had been looking forward to for nearly two years and he savored the moment to the utmost. What could be sweeter in life than the anticipation of battle?

As he marched along, Kataoka's mind, too, was stirred by the killing of the dog. He remembered the funeral procession they had encountered in the streets of Edo on the way to the Shogun's castle with Lord Asano. He was sure it was a good omen. A dead dog was a sure sign that Kira was waiting for them at the end of the road. He only hoped he would be the one to find him first. Kira was an excellent swordsman, he knew, but in his present keyed-up state he felt he could take on twenty Kiras and come out on top. His steel blade ached to slash into the body of his master's betrayer.

The older men marched with more difficulty through the snow, but their step was no less determined. Onodera and Yoshida both saw the events of the night in broader perspective. To them it was like the moves in a game of *go* in which each piece had to play a part. Killing the dog was the first move but it was the overall strategy that was most important and would determine their success or failure.

For most of the younger men, the dog was only a dog, a nuisance that had to be destroyed. Their real test would come when they faced cold steel for the first time. Then they would know, Chikara among them, if they were truly worthy to be called samurai.

As Mimura passed the body of the dog he quickly ducked out of formation to cover it with snow so that it would not be found until the morning sun warmed the ground. Back in line, he looked closely at the snow, as though he had never seen it before. In the moonlight it had never looked more beautiful. He tried to recall a poem about snow but none came to mind; it never occurred to him to try to compose one of his own. That was for nobles and samurai—to match words to scenes of natural beauty. He was only there to do their bidding, although in this case their desires matched his own. There was one other he would like to see die besides Kira and that was the kitchen boy at the restaurant, but a little snow would not cover that over and it was fortunate for all that he was far from the object of his hatred.

Oishi, at the head of the column, had already forgotten the dog. He was busy projecting himself into the minds of his adversaries, trying to imagine how they would react to the attack, wondering if they had a foolproof system for summoning aid.

The greatest single danger was that an alarm would be raised so soon that reinforcements would arrive before they had dealt with Kira. His band of forty-seven was already outnumbered by the sixty archers in the mansion, not to mention the countless servants who would fight if ordered to. But if other forces were committed, either by Chisaka from the house of Uesugi or by any of Kira's neighbors, his men would be bound to be defeated.

Therefore it was reasonable to assume that Kira's first action would be to send for help. He might have signal fires to light, in which case they would have to be quickly extinguished. Or he might try to send a messenger on foot. With Oishi's forces at both gates he did not think a messenger could get through, but if he did it would be only a matter of minutes before the bowmen of Uesugi would be upon them. The question was, could they find Kira before any of these possibilities were realized?

The orders for all were to find Kira without delay, engage in no unnecessary combat and kill no one who did not offer resistance. They knew from their map which room was supposed to be Kira's, but at the sound of an alarm he might head for a safer place.

Oishi shook his head. He had tried to think of everything; he could only hope he had been thorough enough.

But now speculation was at an end. They had arrived at Kira's gate and it was time for action.

Silence was of the utmost importance and no one spoke a word as the pace slowed and finally stopped. There was no sound from within and they assumed that thus far they were undiscovered.

Now Oishi gave the order and his two assault groups formed. Hara led his men to the rear and again listened for signs of activity within. He heard nothing and quickly beckoned to Kataoka, who had been assigned to his party for a very special reason. The monkey-faced little man stepped forward with a grin, spat on his hands, and started up the wall by the gate with a boost from Mimura. He gained the top in silence and, after a careful look around, he leaned back over the wall to assist the next man up. It was young Yato, who was boosted up by Hara and Mimura together; after him came two others. Now the four men on the wall waited until their eyes grew accustomed to the darkness and they could see what the guards were doing. There were two of them in the shadows below, drowsily leaning against the very wall on which the invaders stood, but as yet they gave no sign that they were aware of trouble.

Kataoka raised his hand, then dropped it in a silent signal and all four men leaped at once. They hit the soft ground and sprang on the guards before they could make a cry. Four sharp swords entered their two bodies almost simultaneously and they died without a sound. Kataoka raced to the gate and unlocked it and with the help of the others pushed it wide open. Hara and his swordsmen came through leaving Yoshida and the other older men outside. There were still no sounds of an entry being made at the front gate and Hara hesitated. The impulse to storm the house alone was strong but he forced himself to wait, realizing that an alarm now could spell disaster if Oishi and his men had not yet made it over the wall.

At the front gate the two ladders prepared for the occasion were hoisted into position at the moment when Oishi judged Kataoka had had time to scale the rear wall. With the exception of Onodera and the elders, the rest of the men went up and over. Here, too, the guards were surprised and overcome before they could let out a cry. As they offered no resistance, Oishi had them bound and gagged rather than killed. This took more time than a sword thrust and to make up for it he led his men at a dead run across the open area surrounding the house. He met Hara just in time to prevent him from entering the house on his own.

Now the two groups rejoined and the burliest men were sent forward to batter down the locked door to the mansion. The wood proved to be more decorative than solid and shattered when they fell against it. This was the first indication to those inside that they were under attack and Oishi and his men hurried through the entrance hall and into the rooms beyond to overwhelm the fighting men before they could arm themselves. In the main reception room they found five soldiers of the guard who fell without a sound before the onslaught. The attackers now spread through the rest of the house, anxious to conclude their business before too much power could be brought to bear against them.

Kira woke an instant before a frantic old servant threw open his bedroom door. The sounds of battle reached his ears and he knew with a terrible dread what had happened.

"Master!" the old man croaked. "Your enemies have entered our walls. What shall we do?"

Kira got up abruptly, knocking over a tray which held the remains of his nightcap pot of tea.

"The guards," he muttered, looking around for his sword, "alert the guards."

"They are doing battle now, master," the old man replied.

"Then get out there and help them," Kira said tonelessly as he fastened his sword belt on over his flowing sleeping robe. Then he headed for the door.

As he stepped into the hallway he froze at the shouts and clang of steel, then hurried away in the opposite direction.

"Delay them, you fool!" he shouted over his shoulder.

"Hold them up as long as you can!"

Then he was gone and the old servant wandered dazedly back the way he had come. The idea of his holding up an army of determined young samurai was more than he could possibly comprehend.

As Kira pounded bare-footed down a remote hall at the rear of the mansion, he nearly ran into a muscular young servant who stood sleepy eyed in his path.

"You there!" Kira accosted him. "Have any of the enemy come this way?"

"Enemy?" the young man asked blankly.

"The men from Ako," Kira spat impatiently. "Don't you know we've been invaded?"

The servant's eyes went wide in surprise but he showed no fear and Kira grabbed him hopefully by the shoulder.

"I want you to take a message—to the house of Uesugi."

The servant nodded. He understood what was required.

"Tell Chisaka to send his full force! And quickly!"

He hustled the servant to a rear door and looked out. In the darkness he could make out nothing but dim forms in the courtyard and he pushed the young man outside with a ghastly smile.

"Hurry," he whispered. "Hurry and we may yet be saved."

The young man disappeared in the blackness and Kira ducked back into the house. He ran down the hallway to yet another wing of bedrooms and opened the door of one of them without formality. He was about to speak to the occupant when he heard the menacing sound of troops approaching and he quickly stepped inside and closed the door.

Oishi, with Chikara and a small group of picked men, headed for Kira's bedroom, according to the plan of the house they had studied so diligently. On the way they met half a dozen terrified servants, both men and women, and brusquely ordered them out of the house to reduce the confused milling around in the hallways.

In the sleeping quarters Oishi and his men yanked open doors and unceremoniously roused more servants and guests, but encountered no resistance. Neither did they find Kira in his room and the search became more frantic as they moved from hallway to hallway.

By now the entire mansion was in an uproar and the screams of the women and the shouts of the men blended with the clash of arms when anyone tried to stand in their way. The actual letting of blood was minimal, however, as there was no attempt on the part of the invaders to kill indiscriminately. Once a foe was disarmed they took no more interest in him; their only concern was to find Kira.

Outside, the pandemonium was just as great. Most of the servants and guests had been routed by now and they milled about bewilderedly in front of the house. The gates were closed and guarded by torchbearers against escape, but the young servant with orders from Kira saw a way out. As quickly as the idea occurred to him, he made a dash for the wall between the gates and leaped for the top in the same way that Kataoka had used to get in. He pulled himself up and over and landed heavily in the street outside.

Onodera, chief of the guard at the front gate, spotted him as he got to his feet and moved rapidly away down a side street. With a shout the old man drew the string of his bow and let an arrow fly but it missed completely, as did the arrows of the other Ako men who were quick enough to sense what was happening.

Onodera immediately ordered two of his men to pursue the escaping servant, but it was hopeless from the start. Besides the head start the boy had, his pursuers were older men and could not hope to match his fleetness. Onodera cursed bitterly that he had let him slip through his fingers. If the boy's intention was to reach the nearby castle of Uesugi, there was every reason to believe they would soon be attacked in overwhelming numbers. Onodera vowed to kill himself or die fighting if his blunder had cost them their chance at Kira.

But now Onodera had another problem. Servants from some of the neighboring houses were approaching in curiosity about the commotion and he had to convince them that this was a private affair. In answer to their questions he displayed the placard that Oishi had prepared:

We, the ronin serving Asano Takumi no Kami, this night will break into the mansion of Kira Kotzuke no Suke to avenge our master. Please be assured that we are neither robbers nor ruffians and no harm will befall the neighboring property.

This seemed to satisfy them and Onodera was relieved to see that none of them took it on himself to go for help. His relief was short lived, however, as the two men he had sent after the servant boy came back exhausted and empty handed. They could only report that their quarry had last been seen running at top speed in the direction of Uesugi's castle.

Inside, the search for Kira went on. Oishi continued his search in the sleeping quarters while Hara's men swarmed through the kitchen and service areas. Chikara had been ordered to stay close by his father and he did his best in spite of the confusion of the search. He was more excited than he had ever been in his life, but he kept as tight a grip on himself as on his sword handle to keep from doing anything that might appear foolish. He was afraid to move ahead of his father for fear of appearing too presumptuous, and unwilling to hang back for fear of looking like a coward. This led to some awkward jostling for position until Oishi worked out a standard procedure for raiding bedrooms. He indicated that Chikara should yank open the sliding doors at the same time that he would step boldly in with his sword raised to challenge those inside. This worked much more smoothly than when both of them attempted to break into the rooms together.

Unfortunately they did not find Kira. There were other nobles present as guests, but none of them offered any resistance and Oishi bypassed them impatiently. They were down to the last few bedrooms when a sudden shout from Hara interrupted them and Oishi led his group off in the direction of the kitchen, leaving Chikara alone to guard the hallway.

Hara had opened a door off the kitchen and run smack into the reserve force of Uesugi's prize archers in their armory. He had barely time to cry out his warning when a flight of arrows was directed at him and he was deeply pierced in the shoulder. The impact sent him spinning backward but with a tremendous force of will he turned back to face his opponents and flung himself at them. By now his men had entered the room behind him and they, too, bore down on the archers who had no time to reload and shoot again under the force of the onslaught. They were forced to draw their swords but in the bloody combat that followed they showed they were not as expert in the use of this weapon, and in a short time every last defender had been cut down.

Hara was breathing hard and the blood was running down the front of his breastplate but the thought of letting up did not occur to him. He had waited for this battle too long to miss any part of it now. He grasped the protruding arrow and snapped it off close to his body so that it would not interfere with his movements and then charged off into yet another room to see what it would yield. His men, inflamed by his example, followed in an all-engulfing wave.

Oishi, summoned by Hara's first cry, arrived in the armory in time to see that Hara had things under control. He had hoped the shout meant Kira had been found, but when he learned that it did not he merely waved at the old warrior without noticing his wound and started back to the sleeping quarters.

Chikara, meanwhile, left alone in the corridor, fretted impatiently. What if Kira were inside one of the few remaining rooms? Wouldn't it be a feather in his cap if he found him and either killed or captured him single-handedly. It was said that Kira was an expert swordsman, but with the confidence of youth Chikara felt sure he could win.

Still, he might have obeyed his father's orders to wait if he had not heard a door slide open in a distant hallway. He hurried in that direction but arrived too late to see Kira, made bold by the silence, race down the hall and disappear out a rear door. As he stood there listening, however, he heard the unmistakable rattle of a sword being buckled on and he found it impossible to stand and wait to be attacked.

He sprang to the door the sounds seemed to be coming from and threw it open. He had not been mistaken about the sword. He found himself staring into the startled eyes of a young man his own age who was fully armed and ready to do battle.

This was Sahyoe, Kira's grandson and successor, although Chikara did not know him by sight. They stared at each other in mutual surprise for a moment and then Sahyoe drew his sword. They lunged almost simultaneously but both blows were parried and neither was hurt. Cautiously they circled each other in the small sleeping chamber, slashing ineffectively at such close quarters. A sword stroke slashed through the *shoji* panels of the wall across from the door and Chikara saw that there was another corridor beyond. He now deliberately swept his sword across the whole wall and ripped out the thin partitions like so many match sticks. Now there was more room in which to maneuver and they made the most of it with bold slashing attacks that turned the room into a shambles. Chikara wanted to call for help but he was determined not to admit he could not handle the situation by himself. His opponent was clearly a more experienced swordsman, and, as Chikara began a slow desperate retreat he hoped that his father would come back in time.

Oishi, on his way back from the kitchen, heard the ring of steel on steel and tried to locate the sounds. They seemed to come from the direction of the garden and he left his group to move in that direction, never dreaming that it was his own son who was engaged in deadly combat. The garden was centrally located and he could see much of what was going on from this vantage point. The sounds that had attracted his attention seemed to come from behind some wooden rain doors directly across from where he was standing.

As he watched he was surprised to see two figures fall with a splintering crash through the doors and into the garden, one on top of the other. He had barely time to recognize the one on the bottom as Chikara when the other swordsman scrambled to his feet and poised his blade for a final thrust.

"Chikara!" Oishi cried out in horror and the swordsman's attention was momentarily diverted. In that split second Chikara rolled to one side, slashing blindly with his own weapon as he did so. He caught the other man a solid hit on one leg and he fell like a cut-down tree. Chikara sprang to his feet and was about to deliver a death blow to the man moaning on the ground when Oishi stopped him.

"Wait!" he called, as he ran to the boy. "He's no danger to us any more."

He kicked Sahyoe's sword away from his reach, recognizing the crest of Uesugi on it as he did so. He pointed to it and Chikara nodded. Then Oishi clapped his son on the back in congratulations for his good showing and they hurried back into the house in search of their prime objective.

Here they rejoined Oishi's original group and finished going through the sleeping quarters. Unfortunately, they found no one left in the house. Every closet had been examined, but of Kira there was no sign. As they finally left the house by a door at the rear they met Hara and his group who had been equally unsuccessful.

Oishi and Hara stood indecisively for a moment until Oishi noticed that his old friend was bleeding from the wound in his shoulder. When he looked closer and saw the broken arrow shaft he called for a torchbearer and ordered Hara to submit to treatment. Hara scowled and was momentarily defiant but then his face went pale as Kataoka set about trying to get the arrow out.

Oishi was close to despair. After all the waiting were their efforts to be for nothing? How could Kira have escaped them when every entrance was guarded? He felt a great depression begin to settle over him as, for the first time, he contemplated the possibility of failure.

Hara fumed with the same sense of futility and as the arrow was pulled from his shoulder he gave vent to his feelings in a mighty shout of pain and anger.

"Kira! Are you a rat that must be smoked out of your hole? Come out and fight like a man!"

There was silence for a moment and then a muffled cry drew everyone's attention to a small wood storage hut near the kitchen entrance. Slowly the door swung open and Oishi held his breath in a silent prayer. Then Kira, in his white sleeping robe and holding his long sword, carefully stepped out. Hara's threat of fire had done the trick and Oishi exhaled in a triumphant sigh.

After a quick glance around told him where he stood, however, Kira surprisingly sprang into a strong posture of defiance and shouted into their faces.

"Come on all of you—I'll take on the whole pack! How many are there? A hundred? I'll take those odds if they're the best you cowards have to offer!"

Whether his challenge came from real courage or was only a trick, it stopped the men of Ako. Even Hara was speechless in the shocked pause that filled the air. Then Oishi took a step forward.

"Let no one interfere," he said. "My 'pack' won't kill you, Lord Kira—but I will."

With a blood-curdling cry Kira lunged at him. Oishi parried his blow and the fight to the death began. As they circled and slashed at each other Oishi deliberately cut Kira's robe away from his shoulder and the scar of the wound made by Lord Asano nearly two years ago became clearly visible in the early light of dawn. At the sight of it the men watching shouted in anger. It inflamed them as it did Oishi and he fought on in cold fury. The scar was a symbol of what they were there for and gave every slash an added significance.

Kira was no easy opponent; he was a good swordsman and made every blow count, but years of soft life in the court eventually began to tell and his breathing became labored. Knowing that he stood alone and that no help could arrive in time to save him, he continued to fight on. If he did not know how to live, he at least meant to show that he knew how to die. His eyes glazed over as his breathing became more painful and suddenly, as he parried yet another hard thrust, he slipped and fell to his knees. His sword stuck in the ground and as he desperately pulled at it he realized his end had come.

"Asano!" he spat, and then died as Oishi, in cold rage, swung his sword with two hands in a great swinging arc which snipped Kira's head from his shoulders. A great cheer of relief and triumph broke out from all the men of Ako and Oishi relaxed to smile wearily at those around him.

"We've done it...we've done it," he murmured and felt with the others that all their sacrifices had been worthwhile. Triumph was theirs and it could never be taken from them. But to conclude their business properly, Oishi knew there was more to be done and he gave the order for his forces to form.

Onodera now came forward with an apologetic account about the escaped servant, but if he expected to be reprimanded he was mistaken. Oishi merely nodded gravely and thanked him for keeping the gate against outsiders for as long as he had.

Kira's bloody head was wrapped in a sleeve of his robe and tied to the point of Mimura's spear which he held high in front of him as the group marched out. All were present; none had been killed, although six men were wounded, including Hara, and the pace was kept deliberately slow to accommodate them.

Some of the men were inclined to relax and joke now that Kira had fallen, but Oishi was thinking of Uesugi's forces and strictly called them to order.

"Make fast your helmet strings when you have won victory," he told them. "We have fought a skirmish, but we may yet have a battle on our hands."

The snow was beginning to fall again in the early morning as they began the long march across the city to Sengaku-ji. On this part of the mission they stayed to the back streets and alleys as much as possible, determined that nothing should interfere with the final act of their plan.

When they reached the little graveyard at Sengaku-ji, the men assembled bareheaded in the falling snow while Kira's head was washed and offered before Lord Asano's tomb. Incense was burned and Oishi placed his dirk before the grave, pointed toward the head and asked his lord to satisfy himself. Then he kneeled and bowed his head to the ground. As the others joined him in bowing deeply to the grave and repeating their own vows of loyalty, Oishi was conscious of a strange calm within himself. He took it to mean that Lord Asano's spirit was satisfied at last and could leave off wandering the earth. Now that justice had been done, his spirit could go to join his ancestors.

They now bowed in final farewell and withdrew into the temple itself. The abbot awakened in fright to find himself surrounded by armed men and when Oishi informed him what they had done, he sent two of the temple priests to put Kira's head in a box and return it to his house. Oishi made it plain that they were asking no favors in the way of sanctuary; they were only waiting there until the Shogun's government should act on the matter. He wrote a report of the whole affair including all their names and designated Yoshida to carry it to the censorate. There was now just one more thing to do before they were arrested. He wrote a note to Lord Asano's widow informing her of their success and asked Yoshida to drop it off on his way to the palace. Now all of his accounts were settled and he was content to be judged.

Chapter Twenty

WHEN LORD SENGOKU, the inspector general, was notified by Yoshida that vengeance had been taken for Lord Asano,
he dressed for a quick inspection of Kira's mansion and then
hurried, white faced, to the Shogun's palace. Yoshida was
allowed to return to Sengaku-ji, where he reported to Oishi
that an emergency session of the Shogun's councilors had
been called. He also reported that although Lord Sengoku had
naturally been shocked by Kira's violent death, he had been
courteous at all times and even seemed a little in awe of
Yoshida himself, as a man who had participated in such a dar-
ing undertaking.

It was late in the day when Yoshida returned but they were
to wait even longer for official action to be taken. It was dark
before a messenger arrived with the word that they were to
be taken to Lord Sengoku's mansion until final disposition
could be made of their case. A short time later the stern-faced
Lord Sengoku himself arrived with a company of seven hundred armed warriors, and Oishi and his men were asked to
assemble.

No force was used against them and they were not treated
as prisoners in any way as they lined up to march again. They

walked proudly out of Sengaku-ji, two by two, with Oishi and Chikara in the lead. The six wounded men were placed in palanquins which were carried by their fellow warriors. In spite of the hour, spectators assembled from nowhere and lined the way in silent respect.

At Lord Sengoku's mansion the band was received with open admiration and treated to a lavish supper. It was long after sundown and this was the first food they had eaten all day. After they were assigned to comfortable sleeping quarters, Oishi expressed his gratitude to their "host" for such excellent care and was told warmly by the ramrod-stiff inspector general that it was only what they deserved.

At the castle of Uesugi, the situation was by no means so tranquil. Summoned before the trembling old Lord, Chisaka was on his knees explaining for the tenth time why he had not sent troops to Kira's aid, each time becoming more flustered and less sure he had done right.

"The servant reported at least one hundred enemy troops—that most of the guards had been killed. I was only thinking of protecting your good name..."

The old Lord of Uesugi grasped his hands together to keep them from shaking so much.

"But why didn't you call me? In a matter of such importance, why did you take so much on to yourself?"

"It was only to save you the nuisance, Your Lordship," Chisaka replied lamely.

Lord Uesugi continued to look down at him with shifty eyes. He knew now, too late, that he had given too much authority to this ambitious little man. He cursed himself for his own indolence, but it was too late to change things now. The damage had been done.

Chisaka hastened to add a few more words in his own behalf.

"I reasoned, Your Lordship, that if I sent troops they would find Kira already dead and if the servant's story was to be even half believed, many more of our brave warriors would be sacrificed as well."

Lord Uesugi made no sound but a sigh so Chisaka continued.

"I think you will also find, my Lord, that there will not be many to mourn the late Lord Kira. He made many enemies during his time in office..."

Chisaka would have gone on but he was interrupted by the arrival of a servant with a message for Lord Uesugi. Chisaka was disturbed to see that his pale-faced master turned even whiter when he read the note. Then he asked the servant to show the visitor in.

"A messenger from the Shogun's council," he muttered nervously.

Chisaka rose to his feet as the messenger entered and unrolled an official scroll. A premonition of disaster swept over the little chief councilor, but he shook his head and leaned tensely forward so as not to miss a word.

"In the matter of the assassination of the Shogun's late Master of Ceremonies," the messenger read tonelessly, "the following official decrees have been made in accordance with the laws of the Shogunate.

"First, Lord Kira's grandson, Sahyoe, having failed to fight to the death in defense of his kinsman, is ordered to disembowel himself as soon as he is physically able.

"Second, any of Lord Kira's retainers who are known to have fled without fighting are to be beheaded if they are of samurai rank, and to be cast adrift as lordless men if they are of lesser rank.

"Third, the Lord of Uesugi," and here the messenger paused to swallow hard, "the Lord of Uesugi, because he did not intercede on behalf of his relation by adoption on the occasion in question, is to have all his domains confiscated forevermore."

The messenger went on to read the official validations to his document, but no one heard him. Lord Uesugi had collapsed in a dead faint and Chisaka, fallen once more to the floor, had such a ringing in his ears that he knew for sure the end of the world had come.

The next morning the men of Ako were divided into four groups and sent to stay in the local mansions of the lords of Hosokawa, Hisamatsu, Mori and Mizuno. Here they would stay until such time as their punishment would be fixed and carried out. Although he would much have preferred to keep his friends with him, Oishi felt obliged to designate Hara, Kataoka, and Horibe as the leaders of the other three groups. He was sure of their ability to deal with any situation and knew he could count on them to set examples for the other men. He shook each one by the hand as they left, knowing the chances were great that he would never see them again. Hara and Kataoka were last and a lump came into Oishi's throat as he bade them farewell. Hara was solemn but Kataoka forced a grin. "We'll meet again," he said, "in the next world if not in this." Then they were gone and the long waiting began. The days passed slowly with alternating rumors of leniency and harshness of sentence, but Oishi had little interest in keeping up with the latest reports. He was content that he had carried out his mission to the best of his ability and was ready to die at any time.

There was one unexpected visitor. Late one winter afternoon Oishi was visited by the tall, distinguished-looking Araki, who had carried the original petition for restoration of the castle to the Shogun's councilors. Araki was anxious to report that from all appearances the government officials concerned did not think Oishi and his men were entirely in the wrong. From Araki, Oishi also learned for the first time of the fate of Sahyoe, Lord Uesugi, and Chisaka.

He thanked Araki for the news, although he did not really think such decisions would have any effect in his own case. The Shogun was merely displaying complete impartiality in the matter of enforcing the feudal code. Oishi and his men had broken other provisions of the same code by taking revenge into their own hands, and he expected they would suffer similar consequences.

Araki further informed him that there was tremendous public sympathy on the side of the men from Ako and that this was undoubtedly causing the delay in their sentencing. The Shogun had even taken the unprecedented step of asking for ballots among the daimyo and consulting other learned men to be sure of doing the right thing. As grievous lawbreakers, guilty of flagrantly disobeying the edict against taking revenge, they were clearly liable for the death penalty, but circumstances seemed to dictate that they not be executed as common criminals. Since they had surrendered the castle at Ako peaceably, it was also accepted that they had shown no personal malice toward the Shogun.

"So how do matters stand now?" Oishi asked with more show of interest than he felt. "Does it look like we will be executed or exiled or imprisoned with torture? I can't see how the sentence could be any less severe."

"There is one hope," said Araki gravely. "The Shogun is conferring with the Abbot of Ueno, the highest authority of Buddhism in Edo. It appears that Tsunayoshi wants him to intercede."

Oishi let out his breath in a long sigh. "I had no idea we'd become so important."

"The whole country is talking about you," said Araki, surprised that Oishi seemed so oblivious of his own fame. "They're even performing plays about you and your men in the theaters of Osaka and Kyoto."

"Kabuki plays?" said Oishi, aroused now to think that their deeds should be imitated by the common players he had seen in the theater.

"What's the matter with that?" asked Araki. "Where else can our noble traditions be so effectively held up as an example for all?"

"Even the peasants,..." muttered Oishi.

"Even the peasants," agreed Araki. "You and I know they are not capable of maintaining the eternal self-discipline of a samurai. But does it do any harm to let them see the examples of their betters and to *try* to emulate them in their own lives?"

"No, I guess not," admitted Oishi, and then he smiled. He knew someone who would be surprised and pleased to hear him make that statement.

Tsunayoshi's interview with the Abbot of Ueno was short and produced little in the way of results. The Shogun, a stickler for etiquette, the protector of dogs, and the unregenerate admirer of young boys, was troubled that he would have to execute such brave men for living up to the feudal code as they saw it, but the venerable old abbot could not help him.

"There is a well-known law against the taking of revenge," the gray-haired priest gently reminded him. "And think of the possible consequences if we allow those who flagrantly break it to go free."

"I didn't necessarily mean to set them free," Tsunayoshi put in nervously. "But as the spiritual leader of the country, if you could recommend leniency..."

"But I cannot," the Abbot said. "I am as bound by the law as you are. There is nothing anyone can do."

Tsunayoshi stood silently for a moment, then bowed and left. At this stage there was truly nothing anyone could do. Except for making one slight alteration in the sentence. This was within his authority and would better serve his own sense of justice.

Early in February the four daimyo who were keeping Oishi and his men in custody were notified that sentence had finally been passed by the Shogun's Council and that representatives of the censor's office would be sent to carry it out. Lord Sengoku immediately notified Oishi that even the Abbot of Ueno had felt powerless to do other than to let the law take its course, and they were accordingly sentenced to death.

Oishi nodded. This was what he had expected all along. But he was due for a surprise when Lord Sengoku told him the manner in which they were to die. Although lordless men and hence not legally entitled to such treatment, they were to be allowed to disembowel themselves in the noble ceremony of seppuku. Oishi could hardly believe his ears and fell forward in a deep bow of gratitude to Lord Sengoku. Then he hastened to tell his men the good news.

On the appointed day, the censors arrived and the men were summoned one by one to platforms outside their respective reception halls. Oishi was to go first, followed by Chikara, and then the rest of the men in order of rank. Oishi bade them farewell and shook their hands with a proud smile. He spoke to Chikara last, but in exactly the same crisp soldierly manner as he had to the others. Then he stepped outside.

It was a clear cold winter's day, much like the one on which Lord Asano had died. Oishi thought of this as he walked slowly and with dignity to his place on the platform before which the ceremonial dirk was laying. He thought, too, of his wife's tears and of Okaru's laughter and of his son's bravery and of the limitless loyalty of such men as Hara, Kataoka, Mimura, Yoshida, Onodera, and the rest. Then his mind came back to himself. There was only one thing left now and he would have done all that was expected of him. As he poised the dirk for the last swift thrust he thanked the gods of heaven and earth for the chance he had had to prove himself as a samurai. In the end this was all that mattered, for a man will only be as long as his life but his name will be for all time.

The men from Ako had defiantly disregarded the Shogun's law, but by dying for their lord they showed their devotion to what they considered the higher morality. A samurai was not taught to revere the Shogun as part of a deliberate policy to prevent loyalty to a lord from developing into a larger loyalty to country and national ruler. It was felt that in this way the Shogun would be better able to maintain his status against the Imperial Court at Kyoto. The wisdom of this policy was proved during the controversy over the restoration of the Emperor in 1868. When the need for a single strong ruler to deal effectively with the Western powers was recognized, many samurai worked against the weakening Shogunate and helped bring about its final disintegration.

The forty-seven ronin were buried at Sengaku-ji temple in a special plot adjacent to the tomb of their beloved master. Lady Asano's tomb is also here, facing the markers of the loyal followers' graves. One can also view the well where Kira's head was washed and nearby there is a museum containing relics of the armor and weapons actually used by the men of Ako.

Sengaku-ji is only a short ride by bus or electric train from the bustling center of Tokyo but inside the temple grounds it is surprisingly easy to go back in spirit to feudal times. The scent of antiquity hangs over Sengaku-ji, as well as the odor of the incense burning before the graves in what has become a national shrine.